The River I Stepped in Yesterday

A Sandhills Legacy

By Lyn Messersmith

Lyn Messersmith

Cover Photos courtesy of Bruce Messersmith
Front Cover: Middle Loup River at Seneca, NE
Back Cover: North Loup River at Brownlee, NE

Library of Congress Control Number: 2019904262
ISBN 978-0-578-46067-3

Other Books by Lyn Messersmith:

Down Wind from the Smoke
Ground Tied
My Sister Mariah
Rumors of the Truth

Printed in the United States by Morris Publishing®
3212 East Highway 30
Kearney, NE 68847
1-800-650-7888

For the families of my heart

Contents

The Rivers

Nebraska is a state of rivers. The Missouri defines its eastern border and the Platte winds through a wide valley that became an interstate for Indian tribes and trappers long before the westering fever began, but there are many smaller rivers which have impacted the lives of residents ever since the first settler put down tentative roots.

Two of those rivers hemmed in the world of my childhood, boundaries that, when crossed, offered a mixture of adventure, celebration, sorrow, and apprehension. The village of Seneca nestles beneath a range of towering sand hills and is bordered on the north by railroad tracks and the Middle Loup River. My best school friend, Elizabeth Avey, lived just north of the river, next to the bridge, and a handful of other dwellings lay to the west of their home, but everything else associated with Seneca began after we crossed the bridge.

Alongside the tracks were holding pens where ranchers drove their cattle to be shipped to the Omaha stockyards. A depot, roundhouse, and café clustered nearby. Aunt Beulah's hotel, home away from home for train crews, cattle buyers, and the occasional salesman, sat across the street from the depot. The two story stucco next to the hotel was my aunt's home, but she rented out the upstairs rooms by the week or month. From there, the town branched off into a hodge-podge of businesses: grocery stores, drugstore, pool hall, movie-theater, power plant, post office, hardware and lumber yard, three churches, and the bank.

At the north end of what passed for a main street, Al Franks sold farm implements and livestock feed. His wife, Agnes, was proprietor of a hole-in-the-wall shop that dealt in women's and children's clothing and various notions. The Franks' were the biggest business people in town; they also ran a mortuary attached to their home a couple of blocks away.

Davitt's harness and shoe repair was next, and the old couple lived in a room at the back. Mrs. D. was the Central operator for the rural telephone exchange. The pool hall was directly across, and the grocery stores were next door. Not much news got by the Davitts.

My Grandma Spencer's house sat half a block from a two story school, which contained grades K-12. Her next door neighbor was the Catholic priest, and across the alley was the jail and auditorium/dance hall. I was scared silly to cut down the alley past the jail if Grandma sent me to the store for something, but that fear was miniscule compared to the terror of looking out her dining room window at the large white building where my first lessons were focused on discrimination between town and country kids.

The school stood sentinel halfway up the hill on the south edge of town. One teacher to a room containing three primary grades was the rule, and rule was the role they claimed, but everyone, including high school students upstairs, knew that Louie Theile was the final authority. Louie rarely left his domain in the furnace room during school hours. When called upon to change a light bulb, unstick a window, or adjust the steam heat, he appeared at the top of the basement steps like a white haired troll and as he shuffled down the hall, unkempt, unshaven, jingling keys and scowling, no child lingered to find out whether he kept candy in an overall pocket.

Much of what shaped the person I became happened south of the river, and I always felt a shiver of anticipation as our vehicle rumbled across the wooden bridge and bumpy tracks. There was excitement for holiday gatherings, dances, and family reunions but, more often, apprehension or sadness at leaving the safety and comfort of our close knit ranching community.

People and places north of the river were the familiar fabric of our daily routines. Here were the kids who accepted me and adults who corrected me, fed me, and bandaged my bruises along with those of their own offspring. I knew the insides of their houses, the hiding places in their groves, and loose boards in their haymows, as well as the names of their dogs and cats, and what the moms cooked for supper.

The North Loup River, beside the tiny hamlet of Brownlee, runs closer to the home ranch where my grandparents established their family, but I was almost unaware of it until my teens. We neighbored more to the west, and most of what we needed was available in Seneca. Once upon a time, Brownlee had been a bustling little town despite having missed the rail lines, but all that happened before the Depression, so when someone spoke of those days it seemed unreal to me.

Roads in both directions were poor but the only real reason for us to cross the North Loup was business in Valentine, fifty odd miles away. Dad occasionally needed to go to the courthouse but Mom and I had no dealings there, so I must have been about ten years old before I saw our county seat.

The rivers have opposite personalities. At Seneca, the Middle Loup hurries along as if it needed to keep pace with the trains. There are fewer bends, and it's deeper, with less quicksand. The North Loup takes its time, takes the bottom along with it, depositing a sandbar every now and then, often changing its mind about those locations. It's mostly knee deep, except where the bottom grabs your feet and sucks you down, encouraging you to take root and grow leaves like the willows that line its banks. Winding through meadows and wide valleys, past ranch buildings and abandoned homesteads, the river seems reluctant to release old times. The rickety bridge at Brownlee has been replaced with a sturdier model, but ice jams still form above it in winter, and kids still swim under it on hot July days.

The bridge at Seneca is newer too, and has moved upstream

4

a quarter mile. It bears a marker to commemorate a young family killed on the railroad tracks several decades ago. Seneca used to have three railroad crossings, and there are other families who might have been memorialized in the same manner. Passenger trains are distant memories now, but the coal traffic has increased, prompting the addition of crossing gates and warning lights.

Old storefronts in Seneca and Brownlee are weathered and abandoned, or have been torn down. One church remains in each village to welcome a handful of worshippers, but the schools have long since closed. Now that cattle are trucked to market, no order buyers roam the country, and train crews are based elsewhere, so there's no need for hotels. These days, we can go to town and back for supplies in less than an hour, but there are no supplies to be had in either place. Stories of the old days would be hard for newcomers to imagine, but there aren't that many newcomers, and even fewer that care to hear those stories.

It's probably true that we can't step in the same river twice. Still, there's a sense of calm and comfort that comes from sitting quietly on the banks as it passes. The rivers remember, and so do I.

Portraits from the Past

I know little of these grandparents whose portraits stare out from ornate frames hanging in the ranch home that my parents built after I was grown. The pictures graced Grandma Spencer's dining room from my earliest memory until her death and then passed to her youngest son, who displayed them proudly, despite his wife's unspoken displeasure.

Ira Spencer died before I was born and few stories of him remain, but that isn't unusual in this family. We tend to leave little behind. His signature on some deeds, a mortgage paid off, some old court records, and a reputation not so much named, as implied, in the hills of his home community; these are the legacies that bring personality to the picture.

Knew his mind, I think. Not afraid to speak it. Stubborn too, no doubt; that's a family trait, but standing ready to help a neighbor in need. Mean, my mother said, but she never knew him either, and her perception was based on the fact that he made Dad quit school in ninth grade to help on the ranch. Mom tended to view anyone who disagreed with her as disagreeable. Dad seldom mentioned his father, other than to reiterate advice passed along about ranching or business practices.

I don't know how many of Granddad's children graduated high school. Thad, his oldest, was a professor at Doane College before moving to Shell, Wyoming to run a saw mill. Fred was a carpenter, but had a reputation as a scholar. The two girls, Beulah and Christine, may not have finished school; that wasn't a priority for women. Claude was known as sort of a rounder. He eloped with Emma Merz, who had been engaged to his brother Fred, and they moved to Wyoming, where he herded sheep and she was postmistress in the village of Shell. Clate and Joe were the youngest, and took on the responsibility of the home ranch.

Perhaps by that time Granddad had decided to retire in town and become a pillar of the community.

Pictures of Granddad have come down to me from opposite ends of his life. The one that hangs in a corner of my den is of a stern looking, elderly gentleman in a business suit, shoulders thrown back and hands clasped behind him. His expression is one of disapproval, although he seems aloof from whatever has caused that emotion. A small photograph from the album which Grandma kept on a shelf under her library table shows Granddad in his late twenties, slender and handsome, with a thick moustache. Here, I note a strong resemblance to my youngest son. Granddad's face is sober and serious, but one has the sense that this is a young man with a head full of dreams and the determination to pursue them.

In the other corner of the den is a matching portrait of Grandma. She's in her fifties, perhaps, hair not yet gray, figure matronly, and posture erect, but then she never got stoop shouldered, even into her nineties. She's standing in the side yard next to her flowers and a small white dog, not smiling, though her eyes are kindly, with a hint of resignation. I know of one or two early photographs of Grandma Lizzie, faded almost beyond recognition, but that too is typical. Men were the ones most recognized, back then. Women knew their place, and kept it, although that didn't mean their influence was negligible. Grandma Lizzie was calm and often silent: the recurring thread in a family tapestry that eventually came unraveled as animosity was fed by jealousy and resentment.

I will never know much about their early lives: how they met, where all they lived before settling here, or even their likes and dislikes, and what kind of education they had. Until recently, when a distant relative from the west coast shared her genealogy research, I didn't even know my grandparents' birthplaces, or whether they had siblings.

For some of us, there's a burning curiosity that comes with age: a wish to know who we are, and why. They're long gone, those who could speak freely but never did. We aren't good with truth, not even now. Pictures offer hints, and ghosts are mostly silent. Ours are no exception.

They Say

This is the sum of my knowledge about Ira and Lizzie Spencer. They came to Nebraska to homestead in the1880's at the invitation of the Eatingers, who had arrived ten years earlier. Lizzie had been an Eatinger; actually she was Elizabeth, but forever known as Lizzie or Lib. They had lived briefly in Arkansas at some point, which I know only because of Grandma's mention of leaving there with everyone weak and sick from the ague, which was another name for malaria. They were in south central Iowa before coming on west, and their decision to migrate may have had to do with expansion of the Eatinger holdings, because their original homestead adjoined Eatingers, but my grandparents later relocated a few valleys north, next to the Merz and Hohstatt families, all of them surrounding Swan Lake.

Eight children were born to Ira and Lizzie. Mark died in infancy, but I don't know where he fit in the lineup. My dad, the youngest, was born in Thedford in 1901. Perhaps Grandma lived there so her children could attend school. I don't know where Dad went to school, only that he always wanted more schooling than he got, and never stopped learning.

Likely they were poor. Mom told me that Dad and some of his friends used to peer in the windows of the church at Christmas, marveling at a tree decorated with tinsel and candles, and children gathered around it enjoying sweet treats. There was no celebration of that kind at his house. He wanted better for me and, whatever else we lacked, there was always Christmas at our home. In later years, Mom sometimes fussed about the mess of pine needles, saying old folks didn't need a tree, but I understood his insistence on keeping Christmas.

I don't know when my grandparents built the home in Seneca where Grandma took in teachers to board after Granddad died. He had helped found the bank in Seneca, and served at least one term as county judge. A court ledger that has come down to our family has entries in his handwriting, and the penmanship and wording indicate he was well schooled.

The older sons were established elsewhere by then, so my dad and Clate, his next older brother, were assigned to manage the ranch. Their sister, Christine, died on her Swan Lake homestead in the 1919 influenza epidemic, leaving no children. Beulah's husband, Roy Vallentine, ran off and left her to raise three boys alone, and she sent them to help on the ranch in summer.

Granddad bred mules, Hereford cattle, and a passel of renegade kids strung out over a quarter century. The mules I know about from neighbors and some registration papers that turned up among deeds to various parcels of land purchased over the years. The cattle were a legacy I grew up helping to tend. His older offspring scattered, some I met only a handful of times.

There were no Christmas cards from Dad's siblings, and very few visits. My parents, and even Grandma Spencer, seldom mentioned them. But, come to think of it, I never heard her mention Grandpa either. Maybe my mother was right about him. One motto of that generation was, "If you can't say something nice, don't say anything at all."

Here Comes the Judge

The tattered ledger containing Seneca's court records hints at more mysteries than it solves, but it makes interesting reading. The first entry is in 1914, the last 1950, but there are gaps that indicate other ledgers were used alternately. Spelling is somewhat innovative, but the language is carefully crafted and liberally sprinkled with legal terms. Signatures of magistrates include my grandfather, Ira Spencer, and reading his entries offer insights into the man I never knew. One mystery...Granddad was obviously well educated, and an early entry identifies him as president of the bank. Why then, would he require his youngest sons to leave school early?

Many of the names of plaintiffs are familiar to me, either from hearing Dad mention them, or knowing their descendants; so I'm reminded that running afoul of the law can be generational. Offenses vary from petit larceny to stolen cattle, horses, hogs, and railroad property, breaking and entering, assault, unpaid accounts, bad checks, and threats of murder. Two offenders were sentenced to sixty days in jail. A note at the bottom of the page reads, "Broke jail. Took door off hinges." No record of the escapees being caught, so maybe the authorities deemed it good riddance.

You can tell when Prohibition went into effect because, for a time, most entries involve being drunk and disorderly, or stills having been raided. Generally no evidence was found, other than a large supply of corn on the premises, or perhaps the law was only looking with one eye. Of course there were whispers of confiscated evidence, so the blank spaces may simply be an effort to cover up an affinity for joy juice on the part of law enforcement.

We begin to note fines for procuring liquor for minors and drunk driving, but not many instances of assault or theft. Apparently citizens were so intent on procuring booze that they couldn't be bothered with much else. Wording of these charges is somewhat creative.

11

"Mr. Drake, whose body is before the court, (makes you wonder how stewed he really was, doesn't it?) is charged with being drunk and disorderly, and causing a public disturbance, which is contrary to the law and dignity of the State of Nebraska." Frequently, the accusation includes "using foul and obscene language in the presence of women and minors." Wouldn't those conservative gentlemen be amazed to know that women and children now use that language publicly? Maybe those really were the good old days.

I don't know if judges campaigned for office or just got railroaded into taking a turn, but they served the community, often lacking any particular credentials, in an effort to make it a safe and orderly place for their families and neighbors. No doubt they risked unpopularity, and perhaps suffered business repercussions, but their values were the glue of any society that isn't ruled by dictators and monarchs. It's interesting that many of those pioneer public servants were ancestors of the community leaders I recall, people my dad always mentioned with great respect. Perhaps it's not only outlaw tendencies that are handed down. And if that should be the case, the responsibilities of parents loom larger than we might have realized.

The City Girl

Someone should have warned her that dreams can be dangerous, especially the ones that come true.

I can picture her blinking into slanting September sun as she descended from the train onto a brick platform next to a depot shaded by a lone cottonwood tree. Most of her worldly possessions, including a contract to teach first through third grades at the Seneca School, were in two shabby suitcases at her feet, but she was one up on her dream. This was the West. Surely the cowboy would appear shortly.

My mother never mentioned first impressions from the fall of 1937 but, given her Omaha upbringing, it must have seemed like she'd stumbled onto the set of a Tom Mix movie. False-fronted stores lined the dusty main street. Saloon, school, gas station, general mercantile, harness shop, drugstore, bank, and a handful of houses in various states of repair constituted the tiny railroad town nestled along a fast flowing river.

She was met by the school board president, who escorted her to a two story yellow house and introduced her to the woman who would give her bed and board, a person of dignified carriage and sober countenance, and to Nellie Thompson, another young teacher with whom she would share a double bed in Mrs. Spencer's unheated spare room.

Mom couldn't have known that this place, and these people, would form the foundation for her adult years. The two teachers began a life-long friendship. My mother and Mrs. Spencer kept an uneasy truce, or at least that's how I came to view it in the years I was party to their relationship.

They got on well enough until Mrs. Spencer's bachelor son came to town. The handsome rancher had escaped matrimony well into his thirties, while squiring many a new schoolmarm to dances and parties, but this time he got tangled in his own loop.

Presently, Mom's black and white dream turned to living color, with hues she hadn't anticipated. The young bride was terrified of horses, but miles of sandy trail lay between her and town, as well as the nearest neighbors, and the only means of transportation involved four legs and leather accouterments. Here were kerosene lamps, an outhouse, a pitcher pump, and recalcitrant coal range in the line shack where, by Dad's own admission, you could throw a cat out the roof most anywhere.

Dad never understood women, let alone one city born. He was baffled by his wife's hankering for nice things, her terror of rats running across her feet while building morning fires, and her frustration at having to rise on winter nights to brush a dusting of snow from my crib blankets. It didn't help that the neighbor women all had wind-chargers to provide a semblance of electricity, telephones that worked, at least sporadically, gas stoves and refrigerators, and even indoor plumbing, although one of them did have to deal with snakes in the toilet.

Neighbors got together for card parties and picnics now and then, but it was a lonely life for young women. The highlight of socialization was brandings, but not for my mom, who, although she played passable piano, wrote lovely poetry, and kept an immaculate house, could barely boil water. Dad was a good plain cook, and taught her the basics, but he wasn't much help when it came to planning a festive meal for all the hungry helpers that showed up on branding day. She got by with a lot of trial and error, and pretty heavy on the error part.

Whatever the neighbor women thought of her at first—and she claimed late in life that bets had been laid as to how long she'd last—they taught her to bake bread, make noodles, can beef, set a hen, darn socks, and deal with disrespectful hired hands. They teased her gently about hands caught in a wringer washer, and a batch of bread that refused to rise. She had buried the dough in the barnyard to keep Dad from knowing of the wasted ingredients, but sun-warmed soil resurrected the mess just in time to greet the hay crew as they put up the horses for the noon meal. That fiasco made her a legend in her time, and her willingness to laugh about it got her accepted in the ranks.

The women took Mom into the circle, brought her to Eastern Star or Women's Club, and initiated her in the convoluted kinship of a community where most of them had been born. But, in her own way, she remained an outsider. She wore housedresses long after the others switched to slacks, polished her nails, broken and torn from peeling mountains of spuds and scrubbing clothes on a washboard, and considered it rude to drop in unannounced. Transplants always struggle to adapt; soil that clings to the roots will have its say about the blooming.

Truth or Dare

My mother must have been frantic. Of course she was frantic about something or other for most of her life, but maybe it began with the knowledge that she was pregnant with me.

It would have been an impossible situation. Her job would end; teachers in those days got fired when pregnant, even if they were married. She'd have to leave behind her friends who continued teaching, face the small town gossip, and the certain disapproval of her future mother in law.

Dad would do the right thing, as a matter of course, but may have had his regrets later on. It took Mom a long time to become the typical ranch wife, and the process was painful for all concerned. They may well have been planning to marry, just not so soon. I will never know this, along with a lot of other details.

And then there were her parents, surely shocked, disappointed in her, and worried about her reduced circumstances and difficult living conditions. Did they offer to let her come home? It wouldn't fit the grandparents I grew up knowing, concerned as they were with social position and appearances. No, she needed to be married.

I never tried to explore the events that made me what I always tried not to be: different, a loner, with a history unmentioned, but unforgotten. Some part of me wants to know now, but if I had the chance I'm not sure I'd want to hear the whole story. This makes me wonder what's wrong with someone so fearful of a truth that's so far in the past it no longer matters. Such reluctance is unworthy of the descendant of a woman who made an uncomfortable bed and learned to lie in it. I inherited a lot from her, but courage wasn't among the things that got passed down.

At Home

I don't recall living in that old house, which was simply three old claim shacks pushed together, but sometime in the early 1940's Dad had a tile block home built. There is a faint memory of watching the workers, but not of moving in.

The new house was a big improvement in some ways; others, not so much, but the design was typical for my dad, who squeezed a nickel till it squalled. It consisted of two rooms, an entry way for hanging coats, and a pantry. The main room was 16x16, and the sleeping room 12x12. There was no electricity, or plumbing, just a pitcher pump at the sink, and the only heat was a coal range which was also used for cooking. I'm sure my mother wished for more space, among other amenities, but it was wartime, materials and dollars were in short supply, and at least she had a roof that didn't leak.

The blocks that formed the structure were plastered on the inside but there was no insulation, and floors were cement, covered by linoleum. Winter mornings found frost thick on windows and in corners of the room. Kitchen fires helped, but floors were always cold, and I learned to spread my toys on an old bearskin rug that Mom laid out in a sunny spot. After meals, if the oven wasn't needed for baking, we'd open it for more warmth, and in evenings we sat around the stove reading, with feet propped on the oven door. Wet mittens were placed there to dry, and putting damp shoes behind the stove assured that they'd be warm when needed, although they stiffened in the drying and were hard to put on. The bedroom was icy in winter, but that was common. Most folks shut off sleeping rooms to save on heat. Everyone piled on blankets, so many it was hard to turn over in bed.

The old shack became a bunkhouse and it took all of our extra army blankets and handed-down quilts to combat breezes that seeped through the cracks and keep hired men from freezing.

Mom put sad irons on the stove to heat after supper. At bedtime they were wrapped in towels and put in our cold beds, one for each of us, and one for each hired man. Some of the neighbors who had fuel oil stoves put outdated Sears and Roebuck or Montgomery Ward catalogs on top to warm, before placing them in the beds. I always liked putting my feet between the pages so as to warm them on both sides.

My best friend, Elizabeth, lived in an interesting house. The one large room downstairs was where all daytime activity happened. It was really more of a dugout than anything, but there was an upstairs, where her parents and four siblings slept in a loft that was curtained off in sections. A tiny room in one corner was just big enough for Elizabeth's single bed, which had a mattress made of hay that crackled when you turned over. I could never make up my mind which was the best thing about spending a night with her, the private room, or a mattress that talked to me, but staying over at her house was something to look forward to. Those adventures always happened in summer, but I imagine the winter nights in that home were a lot like sleeping in our bunkhouse.

One Evening

A kerosene lamp sits squarely in the middle of the bright colored oilcloth covering the heavy oak table which centers our daily routines. The lamp sputters, smokes, and flickers when Mom moves to turn it down. A smaller version burns brightly on the stand by the couch that holds a large battery radio and a few magazines.

I sit next to the radio, on Dad's lap. We lean close to listen because the battery is getting weak. Most times we only keep it on long enough to get the news at noon, and maybe an hour at night. World War Two rationing of food and goods means we never know when we will be able to get a new battery. We mostly hear war news, but Dad also favors prize fights and the Grand Old Opry. I like the Lone Ranger, Fibber McGee, and Gene Autry.

You can tell where Dad sits, even when he's out feeding cattle or putting up hay, because all the springs at that end of the couch are broken or sagging. One or two even poke through the fabric, and Mom tries to cover that part up by keeping an old bedspread over it but it doesn't seem to bother Dad, or me, because I never sit on the couch unless he's home. Then I sit on his lap, or maybe on his shoulders, so I can brush his thick wavy hair. I do this for the sensation of it slipping through my fingers, but also because it's the only time I'm allowed to sit on the back of the couch, which is also broken and sagging in a couple of places.

Tonight is different. I'm learning to read, and it's the most thrilling event of my four short years. It means I'll soon be a grown up like my parents, and Jerry, the hired man. All of them read every evening, and any other time when they aren't working.

Dad reads his paper, the Blucher Boot Catalog, magazines with pictures of cattle, or hunters with dogs and guns. Mom prefers thick books, or slippery magazines with pictures of smiling women on the cover. Sometimes she reads to me out of the book of fairy tales, but I don't like those stories much. They're scary, and the pictures are worse than the words. What I like most are stories about dogs and horses. Jerry reads with a magnifying glass because he lost the sight in one eye while welding. He goes for books with pictures of cowboys, running horses, and bad men with six shooters.

Tonight, I'm struggling to connect letters with the meaning of words, and words to matching pictures in a small pamphlet that shows medals and ribbons awarded for military honors. This is the book I've chosen to read first, because it's tiny and easy to hold, with brightly colored pictures. I hear more war stories than fairy tales anyhow; they're part of my world. The Purple Heart is my favorite. I ask Dad if he has one. He explains he's too old to be in the army, so he helps the soldiers by raising food. That makes me proud, and I know which book I want to read next; the Blucher Boot Catalog! Dad's boots are his prize possession, and in the evenings he takes them off and lets me clomp around the house in them. Someday I'm going to grow into them, and then I'll help the soldiers too.

Bedtime Story

The house is dark, except for the dim glow of one kerosene lamp on the kitchen table. All of us are outdoors, sprawled on the lawn, waiting for the heat of afternoon and supper fires to dissipate enough to sleep with some degree of comfort. But the house won't really cool at all, unless the hint of heat lightning on the horizon develops into enough of a shower to provide a breeze.

Mosquitoes gnaw at our skin, but I avoid the confines of netting my mother has spread over me, and the rough army blanket put down for me to lie on as protection from chiggers. Brushing them aside, I jump up and run to the edge of what passes for a lawn, spread my arms and try to grab a handful of Milky Way. If I could just capture some of that to put in the jar with my fireflies it would make such a pretty, soft bed for them.

I visualize the Milky Way as something like the spun glass called angel hair that Mom puts under our Christmas tree, only softer. I'm not allowed to handle the angel hair. She says it would cut my fingers, but the Milky Way must be more like cottonwood fluff, I think. And it seems reasonable to me that if I've caught fireflies out of summer darkness I'd surely be able to capture a chunk of Milky Way when I get just a tad taller.

The lazy buzz of hired men's conversation blends with the hum of insects, now and then punctuated by a burst of laughter at some grown up joke. From time to time, I plop down and settle briefly in the crook of Dad's arm, letting the smoke from his pipe drive away the bloodthirsty swarm.

Soon, Mom's going to say it's bedtime, but I'm sure it's still too hot in the house to sleep, and hope that the magic in our yard lasts until I drop exhausted onto the blanket, so I won't know when it's over.

Outside

I shiver, fold my arms close against the cold, and shift my weight from one foot to the other in indecision. We're way down in the fall now, and it's not fun out here without my coat and shoes. I can tell the sun is setting because the eastern sky has that pink-gold light that brings anticipation of family settling in for supper, safe from whatever lurks in the scary darkness outside, but this evening is scary even before the dark comes. I go around to the other side of the house to look for the evening star, wanting something to be the same as always, but it's still too light for stars.

Our dog, Rippy, presses close and whines as if she senses the confusion that churns in my belly. Certain that the events of this evening will mean change for all of us, including Rippy, I'm suddenly terrified at the possibility of being without her.

I'm pretty tall for a five year old, but I still need to stand on tiptoe to peek in the kitchen window. I can see the kerosene lamp in the middle of the table, and a teakettle on the back of the coal range. A kettle of soup is there too and I'm hungry, remembering how good it smelled a few minutes ago, before everything turned ugly. I wonder what will have changed when I go back in and how I'll know when it's safe to do that. When the yelling stops, I guess.

I don't know what a divorce is but I have the notion it changes lives, and not in a good way. It must be some sort of a secret because Mom told me to go outside and wait while she asked Dad for one. But the secret I won't learn for some time to come is that people get used to what occurs often, so as these scenarios become routine, they'll lose their power to spoil my supper.

No Promises

"Can we go to the circus, Daddy? Pretty please, can we go?"

"We'll see."

No matter how many times I asked, or how hard I begged for a promise involving some upcoming event, Dad's reply was standard. I was always frustrated, but undaunted. Dad was as consistently noncommittal as I was persistently annoying.

How did I even know there was to be a circus? We had no telephone, and neighbors didn't drop by that regularly. In retrospect, I wonder if Mom didn't let it slip, in hopes I'd take up the campaign and get us off the place for a day of diversion. In which case, I didn't disappoint.

Did I even know what a circus was? Where was it to be held? None of this is part of the memory, other than it was in the nearby town of Mullen, and I got to ride an elephant. Is this the circus where I fed a monkey a peanut and got bitten, ending up at Doc Walker's for stitches and a shot?

The Shrine Circus that Grandpa James took me to in Omaha was a spectacular affair, and surely occurred later, since my recollections are clearer. Cotton candy, a toy baton sprinkled with glitter, balloons, clowns, and a breathtaking trapeze act that made me hide my eyes, certain that the beautiful lady would fall to her death. No, the circus I badgered Dad about was surely my first.

We did go; the proof is there in my scrapbook, in black and white. Dad, with his unruly hair slicked back, Mom in town clothes, and me in a striped dress, squinting into summer sun and grinning all over my five year old self. I don't know who took the picture, maybe a hired man, or the neighbor who gave us a ride to town.

To this day, when I hear the word circus, two others echo in my mind. "We'll see." I would hear them regularly during my growing up years, and even beyond.

"Can Sally spend the night?"

"Are you coming to the Christmas program?"

"Can I go along with you to drive the steers to town?"

"Are we going to the dance on Saturday night?"

"Can I go to the show with Jim?"

Eventually, I learned not to ask too far ahead of time, as the answer never varied, and in reality, "we'll see" usually meant yes. My mother's mantra was that half the fun of an event is looking forward to it, but how can you look forward to something that you aren't sure will happen? I was well along in childhood before I was able to reconcile the different outlooks of my parents, and with that being said, I must admit that I'm still inclined to spend too much time looking forward, which results in frequent frustration when plans must change.

Dad never broke a promise to me, because he refused to make one. As a rancher, he knew to expect the unexpected: blizzards, a heifer needing help with birthing, or hay down and too dry to leave another day. Whatever might happen was his to deal with, even if it meant temporarily breaking my heart. Breaking my heart over those details wasn't nearly as serious to him as having to break his word.

Company's Coming!

My Arizona cousins were coming to visit! I was breathless with excitement—these were cousins I had never met, and from Arizona, that magical land of the cowboy as depicted in movies and books by Zane Gray.

Dad told me that John and Ann had two girls and a boy, all younger than me. John was the youngest of Aunt Beulah's boys, all men, really, although they were mostly known as "the boys," in family discussions.

Spencer and Courtney, John's older brothers, were often at my aunt's. Courtney was single, and kept a room there, but he came and went a lot, occasionally appearing at holiday gatherings with a lady friend.

Spencer had a family of kids; Nick and Jacqueline were about my age and we played together whenever they were around. Roberta and Steve were much younger so I didn't know them well. Spencer's wife, Georgetta, was pretty, and fun to be with, but there was a mysterious aura of sadness in her eyes, which I attributed to the story Mom told me of twin babies buried in the Seneca cemetery. They divorced in later years, so perhaps there was more to the picture than I could see as a child.

John and Ann—pretty names, I thought. And the names of their daughters! I'd never known anyone called Roxanne, and Flame—that name was beyond romantic, even if my mother did consider it foolish. I wished for a fancy name like that, and visualized them as lovely as the fairy princesses in my story books.

Arizona! Would John wear a big white hat like Gene Autry? Have his pants tucked into tall boots, and maybe carry a revolver on his hip?

25

Company always made my mother nervous and she had spent the day fussing around the house, which enhanced my sense that these were my most glamourous cousins. Now the magic moment was at hand, and I was totally prepared to impress, having donned my cowboy hat, western shirt, boots, and even strapped on a pearl handled cap gun.

John was tall and dark, like my dad, but the resemblance ended there. He wore slacks, a short sleeved polo shirt, and oxfords! Well, maybe I'd misunderstood. They weren't from Arizona after all. These people looked more like my city grandparents.

Ann was slender and pretty, in an understated way, with shoulder length brown hair, sort of mousey, like my own. She didn't have much to contribute to the conversation, other than some references to Tucson, where they had recently bought a home.

The boy, Johnny, was of no interest to me, and the girls were prissy little things who clung to their mother's side. We didn't go out and dig in my sand pile, climb trees, or visit the haymow to discover kittens. They didn't even want to ride horses or play with my dog.

I can't recall if I entertained my city cousins, or if so, what we did. I didn't have many dolls, and half the time had left them at the barn, or just misplaced them, so perhaps we simply sat and stared at one another until the grownups shooed us outdoors, where we proceeded to stare some more.

In my memory, the visit was brief, and rather stilted, even for grownups. It was several more years before I realized I'd been surrounded by cowboys all my life, and needn't go looking for them in the movies or faraway places. I did wish my dad and the other ranchers would wear blue jeans instead of the tan work pants they all favored. Still, it could have been worse. They might have put on bib overalls like the old geezers who lounged on the benches outside the pool hall in Seneca.

Family Ties

As often happens, the two youngest of Ira Spencer's clan ended up keeping home fires burning. My dad, Joe, and his brother Clate, were in partnership on the ranch with their mother for my early years. Each brother had his own brand, Dad used the ZX, and Clate had the Hog Eye. There was a ranch brand too, Bar K4, but I don't know if those cattle were shared between the three, or what kind of cut my grandmother got of the deal.

For a lot of my childhood the brothers shared a battered pickup, and most of our travels depended on whether the rig was at our place or the one where Clate and his family lived, in a valley six miles across the hills. What passed for a road to that place mostly wasn't, so we didn't see them much, and it was a treat when Dad took me along to visit my cousins on days when he and Clate had work to do together.

The brothers seemed to manage an amicable relationship despite having opposite personalities. Clate, known as Frosty to his brothers because of having a shock of white hair, was born a century too late. He'd have made a good mountain man. Dad's nickname was Nels, but Clate was the only one who ever called him by it, and no one knows where that originated. Dad was community minded, pretty conservative in his views, and ended up being the one responsible for his mother's interests in her old age.

Clate's wife, Leona, was my favorite aunt, probably because she managed to smile more than she ever had reason to, and their kids, Sally, Betty, and Johnny, were my favorite cousins. Their house seemed pretty grand to me, simply by virtue of having several rooms. I was oblivious to the cracks that let wind whistle through, rough, unpainted boards, and general disrepair, but it's likely that Leona was not. In comparison to his brother, Dad was a spendthrift when it came to creature comforts. Most of Dad's spare nickels went for ranch necessities. Clate's went for a bottle.

I disremember Mom ever visiting at Leona's house, and only a few times when Aunt Lee and the kids came to ours. Looking back, I think the brothers agreed on few things, other than that a woman's place was at home.

The partnership split up when I was in grade school, and Clate bought a ranch east of Brownlee. The roads over there were more conducive to visiting but tempers were not. Most of those dynamics were kept from us kids, and we were clueless to the fact that we were living on the cusp of change. It's likely the adults did us a favor by keeping still about conflicts, but the breakup came with a shock I never quite got over. There had to have been a better way to handle the transition, but no doubt the adults did the best they knew how at the time.

War Paint

The bright red lipstick didn't go on quite like I had planned. I was in a hurry, not wanting to get caught messing with Mom's things. She often let me play with the stuff on her dresser, sifting through the meager stash of costume jewelry, looking at myself in a hand mirror that matched the brush and comb, and opening the gold colored tube of lipstick, dreaming of a day when I'd be all grown up, and could put on lipstick and face powder, along with those high heeled navy blue suede pumps, with open toes, that Mom wore to dances.

Maybe I was nervous because this time I hadn't asked permission to look at her things. Still, what could it hurt? She always said yes when I did ask. Occasionally, she even let me paint my fingernails, but that wasn't nearly so exciting because Mom usually wore clear polish, or a pale rose shade that seemed dull to me. I never could figure out why she wore bright lipstick but stuck to pink nail polish.

There weren't any dangly earrings in her jewelry case either. Mom believed they were inappropriate for nice women, and that went for having pierced ears as well. She could be awfully boring sometimes, but at the moment I was willing to settle for seeing how I'd look in lipstick.

The bedroom was cold. In winter we kept the door shut in order to conserve heat in the front room. Dad wasn't about to carry any more coal for the cook stove than necessary, and Mom felt the same way about hauling out ashes.

Mom must have thought I was in there too long. I guess hurrying is different for a five year old than for adults, or perhaps it was simply a matter of the "too quiet" inner warning that seems to arrive with motherhood. All I recall about being busted is having my face scrubbed until the washrag was candy striped and my skin felt as though the nap on the material had come off on my face.

My cheeks and chin were a rosy red when she finished cleaning me up, but there remained no trace of scarlet on my lips. However, I was beginning to get a smidgen of understanding why it was that Dad kidded Mom about putting on her war paint when she got ready to go somewhere. I hadn't gotten a spanking, but my ego and stinging skin felt a lot like I'd been in a battle.

Another Bedtime Story

There was certainly no good reason to put my head between those bars. I don't even recall considering the deed before it was done, and I had begun to believe it was a bad idea.

Our beds were the old fashioned kind. Well, at the time they weren't all that old fashioned, because everyone I knew slept in beds with tall head and foot boards made of steel pipe. Vertical bars were placed ten or twelve inches apart as reinforcement.

All of our beds had sagging springs under lumpy cotton mattresses which Mom turned every week when she changed sheets. The turning was simply a formal nod to proper homemaking, because as soon as anyone lay down on the bed they would naturally roll to the middle. Not a problem, except when you wanted out, or if there were two to a bed, in which case you were doomed to snuggle, the only other option being to stay in place by hooking an arm or leg over the edge to avoid touching the other person.

Sally and Betty and I often slept three to a bed, and on those occasions our moms had us draw straws to see who had to take the middle. Best case scenario was an outside berth next to the wall, so as to prop against that, and for Betty to get the opposite side, because she tended toward incontinence. When Betty slept in the middle, everyone got damp.

Doubling or tripling kids in a bed was common, but as the number of cousins needing put to bed increased, so did our parents' creativity. Four or five youngsters would fit crosswise, if they were short enough so no one's feet hung over too far. Sometimes we were placed alternately, head to foot, which was okay as long as no one was so tall they kicked their companions in the face.

Grandma Spencer's spare room had a fancy brass bed frame, but the mattress was just as uncomfortable as ours at home. While living with her for school, I preferred the cold nights when she invited me to share her featherbed, even though she snored mightily for such a quiet, unassuming woman.

Not many people know this, but those old iron bedsteads were the forerunners of modern trampolines. Kids shut in on rainy days, or simply bored out of their minds, often perched on the highest end and hammered heels on the cross bars to see who could make the most noise. Tired of that, we launched ourselves off, hoping to land at the foot of the bed without banging our heads. We could usually jump high enough to touch the ceiling at least once before the bed broke and brought an adult screeching down the hall to send us packing.

My parents' tiny house didn't allow for such antics. You just couldn't get far enough from authority to have much fun on the beds, but I did like to spread out paper dolls there, and often hung by my knees from the foot, or straddled it to play horse.

I must have been five or six that summer, and whatever game I had going on a particular day probably required escaping out the foot of the folks' bed headfirst. Almost immediately, I had a second thought. It's amazing that a head which slides through an opening so easily is nearly impossible to withdraw when backing up. The difficulty is exponentially enhanced by the degree of panic involved on the part of the captive.

Obviously my mother solved the situation, but my only memory of the event concerns the certainty that I'd live out my life as a prisoner of the bed.

I've been claustrophobic ever since.

Learning To Be a Grownup

"When you go to school," Mom said, *"you'll be able to read all these stories yourself."*

"What's school?" I asked.

"At school there are other kids to play with. You must mind the teacher, and not make noise. You'll have fun learning to read, and write, and count."

"I'm not going," I said, and as far as I was concerned, the subject was closed.

Mom mentioned school a few more times, but nothing came of it. I knew it'd never happen. It was a silly idea anyway. Mom could read to me. She didn't have any other kids, and we didn't have close neighbors or a car to go visit them, so I wasn't much used to playmates. School was just another one of Mom's silly sayings like, "don't pester the hired man, or he'll quit." I'd pestered him since I was just little, and he hadn't quit yet.

Then Mom started sitting me down every day to do something called lessons. I didn't care much for that, but I was learning to read and write so there was no need to worry about something called school, even if such a thing existed.

Something suspicious was happening. I was given a tablet, pencils, crayons, and a book bag. Mom said they were for school. Grownups get silly ideas sometimes, and you just have to humor them. Everyone knows they say nonsense like, "you look good enough to eat!" No one had ever taken a bite out of me or any of my friends.

Whatever they said about this place called school I knew it was just imaginary. I certainly never had seen one, and didn't know anyone who ever went there, except Mom and Mary's little lamb. The lamb was just a story, and Mom didn't count; she was a grownup. Fairy tales aren't supposed to make sense, so I didn't bother with it.

One day, Uncle Clate came to our ranch in the pickup he and my dad shared. Dad must have been too busy elsewhere, or perhaps Clate was the one needing to get something in town. Mom and I got in and we set off for Grandma Spencer's house in Seneca. It took forever and three days. Mom said about an hour, but whatever it was I hated the trip because I always got car sick.

Mom said I would live with Grandma and go to school. Wouldn't that be fun? I didn't think so, but I was sure Grandma would set her straight, so I didn't argue. Before we were halfway there my stomach was turning cartwheels and I was sure I'd not live long enough to confront the issue anyhow.

We stayed all night at Grandma's. Next morning Mom had me dress in new clothes, and put the tablet and other stuff in the book bag. We walked across a vacant lot to a big white two story building where boys and girls were running around the yard making an awful commotion. Some old folks that looked to be about thirty-seven went up the steps carrying books and acting uppity. Mom said the high school was up there, and some of those people had been her students when they were little like me. Judging from their looks, I decided that was a zillion years ago.

She showed me a little room with chairs that had water in them and told me what it was for. I decided it must be a dangerous place, because she said I was to ask permission before going there. Our neighbors and my grandparents had bathrooms, but I never had to ask to use them. Then we went to a big room with lots of little tables and chairs. There was a wooden trough in one corner with sand in it. Mom would have tanned my backside if I ever brought that much dirt in the house, but this strange lady took my

35

hand and we went over there. Other kids were digging in it and she said I could too.

Mom had said school was for learning to read. I already knew how to read, so maybe they were going to teach me to dig. I already knew how to do that too, but perhaps they had some different ways, and when I learned them I could go home.

When I looked up, Mom was gone. I had a notion to cry but she'd said I mustn't be any bother, so I didn't. But all day long there was this thing like an orange in my throat. I'd had an orange once. It was good, but this tasted salty, and I didn't care for it.

We were sent outside to play after a while. I didn't know any games but the other kids did, and they knew one another's names. I sat on the steps until Teacher came out and shooed me off like Mom shooed hens off the doorstep. The kids started saying things about my clothes and the way Mom had braided my hair. All the other little girls had curls, and they laughed and pointed fingers at me. I wondered if the teacher would come out and tell us when it was time to start having fun.

When it was time to go home, I began walking toward Grandma's. Suddenly, a rock hit me in the back, and when I turned around some more hit me in the face. Some of the kids were yelling about dumb country hicks. I ran. When I got to Grandma's she told me not to be a crybaby, or no one would want to play with me.

Next day I went back. There wasn't much else to do. It was too far to walk home. Grandma said my uncle would come get me at Thanksgiving. Maybe by then I'd have learned all about digging and could stay home.

That day, Teacher said she was putting me in second grade because I already knew how to read and count. I didn't care. It was still the same room, with the same kids. That night when they chased me home they called me Teacher's Pet. I didn't know what that was, but it must be worse than Dummy, because the rocks were bigger. I ran faster and didn't get hit.

Grandma sent me to the store for a loaf of bread. It was a long way, about two blocks, and I had to pass the jail. I was sure the bad people in there would grab me, but then I met some kids from school and the jail looked like a safer place than the street. When I ran back to the house Grandma scolded me. She said if I didn't run, they couldn't chase me.

Well, I knew one thing for sure. School didn't make you smarter. Mom said it would be fun. Teacher said play nice. Grandma said if I didn't run they couldn't chase me. But I didn't run until they chased me. The kids didn't play nice, and if this was Mom's idea of fun she was welcome to it.

Mom, Teacher, and Grandma had all gone to school, and they were all wrong. I might as well make up my mind to being wrong, if that's what you learned there. It didn't look like much fun being a grown up, and I decided I wouldn't do it.

Nothing to Do But Stay

I never noticed how early the sky goes to sleep in October until I moved to town to live at Grandma Spencer's. Not that there's anything calling me outside. I've already poked around in the yard and slid down the cellar door, which isn't much fun unless my cousins are there to do it with. I sat on the front steps awhile, and watched Charlene's house, across the street. She was playing with her friend Shirley, and they made faces at me before going inside. Both of them are a grade ahead of me. Making faces isn't much, at least not as much as the names they call me at school.

There's a lot of activity at that house, but I can't keep the people straight because they all have the same last name and look alike. Charlene has a younger sister; maybe a couple of brothers. There are two younger boys that belong to Charlene's grownup sister, who also lives there. I think she works at the café sometimes, and I don't know where Charlene's dad works, if he does. The mom is dead, someone said, and it looks like no one makes anyone do anything they don't want to, or come home on time. I wonder if I'd like that kind of freedom. It feels like no one really cares where those kids are, or what they do, but at least they keep busy. And Charlene has a best friend, Shirley Devine. I wonder if I will ever have one.

I don't have time to worry about that, though. Grandma just told me to come in and wash up for supper. Now I start wondering what I'll do after that. It doesn't take long to eat our sandwiches. Maybe one reason I'm never very hungry here is that we eat a lot of sandwiches. At home we come in the house at night smelling fried taters and steak, or a pot of soup; even goulash.

When the dishes are done we go in the living room. Grandma sits in her wicker rocking chair and reads a magazine. I avoid the sofa and overstuffed chair that are covered with an ugly maroon fabric that prickles. Nobody sits there unless it's the only place left. Instead, I color pictures, or dig through the drawers in the hall cupboard to find dress up clothes, but dressing up isn't any fun without Sally and Betty here to play it with. Grandma says I can take the magazines off the shelf under the library table and use it for a doll bed, so I do that for a while, but I really don't care much for dolls. Finally I crawl up there myself just to see if I fit, and I do, so I lie there and think about how at home they'd be listening to the radio. Grandma doesn't have one, or if she does, I've never seen it.

Pretty soon Grandma takes up her flashlight and we put on our wraps to go visiting. Sometimes we walk up the hill to see Mrs. Poston, or kitty-wampus across to Aunt Beulah's. None of Grandma's friends have husbands, so it's just boring woman talk. Tonight we go the other way and stop at Mrs. Beals'. I kind of like it when we go there. She usually has cookies for me. I suppose she has to keep them around for her grown son, Art, who lives there too. He sits in the corner with a magazine and doesn't look at us. Maybe he's tired from work, but I never see him go anywhere to work, so maybe he just doesn't like company. The women chat. I sit on the floor and listen, and then we go home to bed.

These nights are so boring and lonesome that I almost look forward to school tomorrow, when I'll see Elizabeth. Of course, there'll be Charlene and Shirley to contend with too, but it still means one more day closer to fall break, when I'll get to go home for a few days. I used to cry myself to sleep, but that didn't make time go any faster, so now I just watch and wait. There's nothing to do but stay.

On to Omaha

Our voices echoed off the walls of the Seneca depot, mingling with the tap-tap of the telegraph machine, bouncing around like popcorn in a skillet. The agent huddled in his cubby-hole as if hiding from the barrage of sound, a green celluloid visor pulled low on his forehead against the glare of overhead lights.

It was always bright in there, either from sun streaming in the large windows on three sides, or bare bulbs hanging from the high ceiling, but I was never in that depot when it felt warm. In winter, the pot-bellied stove didn't make much of a dent in the emptiness enclosed by cement walls, which also kept out most of summer's heat.

Number 44 arrived in early afternoon, and it was this train Mom and I usually took to visit my grandparents in Omaha. If, for some reason, we happened to depart on 42, in the middle of the night, Mom would make me a bed on the hard benches by padding them with our coats. "Sleep now,'" she'd say. "It's a long time before the train comes."

I never did doze off. It was too cold, the bench too hard, the light too bright, and I was too excited. I'd sleep on the train, where lights were dim and the rocking motion made my eyes heavy.

We were generally the only ones waiting to board, but now and then someone else was on hand to make conversation with Mom, who sat alert and upright, dressed in her city clothes complete with hat, gloves, and high heeled pumps.

It was easy to tell when the train was coming. First I heard a faint rumble, which grew louder until the ground shook. When the whistle screamed at the west crossing, we took up our bags and went out on the brick platform. I hid behind Mom, clinging to her skirts as the noise grew and seemed to engulf us. Then came the most terrifying sound of all; a burst of steam escaping, and a squeal of brakes as the engine pulled past and rolled to a stop. Mom fussed at me for being such a baby, reminding me that loud noises never hurt anyone, and the train couldn't get me because it had to stay on the tracks. Prior experience had proved her right, but I couldn't afford to take any chances, so she always approached the passenger cars with a gait resembling that of someone in a three legged race, while struggling with our luggage. I wouldn't let go of her skirts until the conductor reached for my hand to help me up the steps.

Those old steam trains stopped at every little town from Seneca to Lincoln, for mail and passengers to be loaded or unloaded. Actually, it was from Alliance to Lincoln; then as now, Alliance was the terminal of origin. Leaving Seneca in the afternoon put us in Ravenna at suppertime, and here there was a twenty minute stop for folks to run uptown and grab a sandwich at the café. Mom never wanted to do that, for fear of missing the train, or perhaps she just didn't want to have to drag me past the engine again. In any case, we always carried a lunch to eat in our seats.

By the time we reached Lincoln it had been dark for hours. Getting off the train wasn't as scary as boarding, probably because of the distraction of a busy city depot. I gazed wide eyed at the travelers hurrying, waiting, meeting new arrivals, or saying farewells. Many of our trips were in wartime, or shortly after, so men in uniform were everywhere, arms around girls in short skirts and high heels, or lounging against a wall, cigarettes dangling from a corner of their mouths, making conversation with buddies seated on sea bags. But it was the occasional black face that caught my eye, because there were no Negroes in our community at that time. Mom scolded me for staring, saying it made them uncomfortable, and besides it was rude.

We had an hour layover in Lincoln. After the war ended,

41

Mom's brother and his wife lived there, so sometimes Aunt Betty and Uncle Vance came down to the depot to visit with us until the Zephyr was announced, and we boarded for the last leg of the trip to Omaha. This boarding was less traumatic, as the Zephyr ran on diesel and was much quieter. True to the name, the remainder of our journey flew by.

Our local trains were seldom crowded. A few folks got on or off at small towns, more at Broken Bow or Grand Island, but except for times when a large group of soldiers were aboard, there were lots of empty seats. This wasn't the case on the Zephyr. More than once, a soldier stood to give Mom his seat, while another dandled me on his knee and told me stories.

Grandpa and Grandma James always met us at the depot in Omaha, and as soon as our bags were stowed in the trunk of their car Grandpa turned to me and said, "How about we go see the lights?" That's unless I had beat him to it, with a query about whether it would happen. Off we went, through the neon of downtown, where familiar landmarks were pointed out: the Orpheum Theater, Brandeis Department Store, the Telephone Building where Grandpa worked, and so on, until we came to Lee's Drugstore on the corner of 55th and Leavenworth, just five blocks from my grandparents' home. I was thrilled that Grandpa had planned this grand tour in my honor, and clueless that it was the shortest route home from the train station.

There is a dim memory of one visit without the lights. Grandpa's car was one of very few on the streets, and no neon was in evidence. When we reached the house, Grandma hurried to pull the blinds and then turned on one small lamp. Mom explained the city was in a blackout, because the Japanese might fly over it and be able to tell where to drop bombs.

For some reason, this didn't give me nightmares. I was well aware of war; Dad listened daily to the news and was adamant that no conversation be carried on during the broadcasts. I knew why we didn't get new shoes, and that sugar, gasoline, and tires were rationed. I'd memorized all the medals for military personnel in a small book on Dad's desk, been shown pictures of the type of plane Uncle Vance flew, and knew names of local boys who were away fighting, but the thought of any of that coming to our doorstep seemed ludicrous to me. The noise of steam engines and Grandma James' vacuum cleaner was a much more certain peril.

Snapshots

Visiting the Omaha grandparents was like stepping into another world. There were different rules for almost everything. Here were lace tablecloths instead of oilcloth, polished silverware placed on both sides of pretty china plates, plush carpets, and sheer curtains. The noon meal was lunch, dainty sandwiches served on small plates in the kitchen, but with dining room manners. Dinner was at suppertime, complete with cloth napkins in rings, individual salt cellars, and formal conversation after Grandpa said grace. Well, it was formal for as long as Grandma could keep control, but she had married a man who liked his fun. He tended toward practical jokes like slipping plastic ice cubes containing a fly into the water glasses, and frequently began a long windy tale for my benefit with the words, "When I was a little girl..."

On these occasions, Grandma gathered up her dignity and scowled at him. "Now Ernest, don't be so foolish." He would settle down then, but not without a conspiratorial wink in my direction, a promise to continue the foolishness when Grandma wasn't around. I used to wonder how the two ever got together, he with his fun loving ways and she, determined to preserve decorum at all costs.

Grandma James was round. Her face and figure matched in that way. Short, plump, arms and legs completed the impression that there was a lot of power here in a pretty small package. At barely more than five feet, she stood straight and looked you in the eye. She must have been a pretty young thing, tiny and pert. Even as a matron she had style. I never saw her in low heeled shoes, even her bedroom slippers were fussy pink replicas of the stylish footwear she favored. Her housedresses were starched and covered with an apron. She wore her medium brown hair in a short, wavy bob reminiscent of the roaring twenties, which suited her well, and favored red lipstick with matching nail polish on well-manicured hands. She wore rubber gloves to do dishes and housework, and in retrospect, I imagine that my mom's work worn hands with broken nails and enlarged knuckles were a trial to the mother who took such pride in maintaining a ladylike image. On our visits to Omaha, we never left the house to go shopping, to church, or for a Sunday drive, without Grandma reminding my mom to put on gloves and a hat.

Grandma was opinionated and sharp of tongue at times, but she had a pleasant manner and the ability to make people comfortable. She smiled frequently, but I don't recall ever hearing her laugh out loud. By contrast, Grandpa was tall, at least for his generation, and slender. I don't recall his hair, or what there was of it, as anything but gray. He laughed easily and teased a lot. Grandpa would have been a good farmer. He liked to garden and work outdoors, and often puttered in the garage. They were an odd couple in a lot of ways, but somehow seemed to fit easily with one another in spite of the differences.

Grandpa turned me into a moon worshipper. He kept track, and when it was full, carried lawn chairs to the back yard so we could bask in the beauty. To this day, when turning calendar pages for a new month, I check to see when the moon will be full. Mom seemed to share this fascination, and I think the ability to view a full moon without competition from city lights was one of the things that eventually turned her into a country woman.

The main bond Mom had with her mother was shopping. Often, during our visits, Grandpa took the bus to his office downtown so we could have the car. Mom and Grandma, decked out as carefully as if for church, crammed me into a dress and hit the streets. My mother was determined to acquire the trappings of civilization, in hopes, I think, that some of it would rub off on me. I have to say that very little did, and I'm unrepentant about that.

My memories of those excursions are blurred—Mom stepping smartly toward Brandeis or Penny's, Grandma's short stride matching mine; both of us six steps behind, with Grandma

45

calling out, "Wilma, for heaven's sake, slow down!"

Dressing rooms, where I fidgeted while Mom tried on clothes, or worse, made me do so. Elevators, escalators, bustling sidewalks, hard faced clerks behind counters of sparkling baubles, and stops in public restrooms where the mantra was always, "Surely you have to go. Just try!" Usually I didn't, I wouldn't, and threw a pretty large tantrum to distract those silly old women.

I did like the cafeteria where we ate lunch, and being able to choose my food, rather than eating what was set before me. It was a nice change from the formal setting I'd have to endure at supper. Oh, sorry. I meant, *Dinner!*

Sometimes Grandma's sister Iva came to dinner. There were never two siblings more different in temperament. Aunt Iva had worked her way through nurses training then married a man who earned his living as a salesman on the road, and died young. She continued to work at Methodist hospital, a necessity to stay afloat financially, although she loved her work, and her patients. Her rusty old car was quite a contrast in the driveway behind my grandparent's shiny one, new every few years.

Aunt Iva was the only one in that family with a nickname. Most people called her Banny, derived from her maiden name of Banfield. She loved to laugh, and had an earthy sense of humor that Grandma did her best to ignore. Often Aunt Iva came directly from work, her white uniform as wrinkled as her tired face. If she'd had time to change to a cotton housedress, she put on carpet slippers and kicked them off as soon as she sat down, rubbing her bunions while saying, "A nurse never stands when she can sit, or sits when she can lie down."

The sisters were alike in that both were opinionated and outspoken, so dinner discussions were lively. They fussed at one another in a friendly way while Grandpa carved the roast. I could tell that he was silently cheering his sister-in-law on, and likely envious of the way that Iva put Grandma in her place; something I never heard him try to do, but woven around all this was an undercurrent of love; the assurance that differences in opinion weren't going to divide the family, and this was a game they enjoyed playing. After her sister had said good night and closed the door Grandma often sighed and said, "I wish Banny didn't have to work so hard."

Hanscom Park Methodist Church was the center of my grandparents' social lives. My impressions of it involve dark polished wood, a pipe organ played so loudly it scared me, dim light filtered through stained glass, and being banished to Sunday-School, where, scrubbed raw and arrayed in a starched, scratchy dress, I sat in a circle of little red chairs among children I'd never seen before, and didn't care to again. I endured the hour in sulky silence, and colored sloppily on a handout that had pictures of people in sandals and bathrobes. Eventually Mom collected me and ushered me into the sanctuary for the sermon, where I prepared to be bored some more. It seemed to be a requirement to linger on the church steps after services while my grandparents greeted acquaintances and showed us off.

"You remember our daughter, Wilma? This is her daughter, Lyn."

After the chin chucking and cheek pinching, we went to Sunday Dinner, which occurred at one o'clock, alternately at Aunt Iva's or my grandparents' home. Occasionally we ate out, but that was rare. Grandpa's middle name was frugal, and he may have respected his son-in-law for that shared characteristic. I never did deduce how "Dinner" at night during the week, became "Dinner" at mid-day on Sunday.

Most Sundays, after the dishes were done and dinner had settled, Grandpa inquired, as if it had just occurred to him, "Who wants to go for a ride?" It wasn't really a question, and whether or not we cared for the notion, no one ever turned him down. The four of us, or five, if Aunt Iva was present, would settle in for an hour of meandering out to Blair, past Boys Town, through Elmwood Park, or some area of the city where new construction was underway. There wasn't much for me to do except listen to the adult conversation or look out the window, which is hard if you're short and sandwiched between two plump ladies in the back seat. My mother usually got to ride in front. ("Go on Wilma, you have long legs like your dad...")

There is no memory of a Sunday drive on the few occasions that Dad was present, but he may not have ever been there on a Sunday. The only times he went to Omaha were when he rode the caboose of a cattle train to market our steers at the Omaha Stockyards. If we went out to eat on Dad's dime, it was always at Johnny's in south Omaha, which was a frequent hangout of all the cattlemen. Grandpa and Grandma wouldn't have chosen that venue on their own, partly because it was swankier than their taste, and partly because it contained a bar. I don't know if Dad visited my grandparents on the trips when Mom and I were not there, or stayed with them. Much as he would have liked to save the cost of a hotel, it's more likely that he stayed downtown at the Castle Hotel, which catered to the stockyard trade. There were, and still are, whispered rumors of high old times at the Castle during the fall shipping season.

I suppose what kept me from being bored on these Sunday outings was the fact that the adults seemed so genuinely interested in mundane things like a new office building, or the mall that was going in out on 72nd Street. "Who in the world would drive clear out here to shop?" my grandma wondered aloud.

I didn't participate much in their conversations, but then I was a pretty silent child. Offering an opinion meant having to defend it, and since no one was going to out argue Grandma there

48

was no point in it.

There wasn't much more for me to do at Grandma and Grandpa James' house than there was at Grandma Spencer's. If it was Saturday, Grandpa let me help polish our shoes for church. We sat at the top of the basement stairs while he applied the different kinds of polish and then I got to brush each pair. This seemed pretty uptown to me because he had a regular kit of brushes and such. We seldom polished shoes at home and, if we did, we just used an old rag. Grandpa washed the car next, another thing that interested me because we didn't have a car, and when we finally got one, washing it was not on our calendar.

They kept a box of toys for me in the front closet, but I soon tired of those and spent most of my time sitting on the front step. At home I would have been out playing around with the cats and dogs, but there wasn't an animal to be seen here, other than a yappy little dog that lived next door and came out of the house only on a leash. No trees to climb, and only a small patch of lawn to walk around on. I liked when Grandpa or a neighbor mowed the lawn, because the scent of fresh cut grass reminded me of the meadow at the ranch. But we never mowed lawns at home. Grass either grew or didn't, and when it got long Dad chopped it back with a scythe.

Mom and Grandma spent the days when we didn't go shopping chatting, mainly about my dad's failures to live up to their expectations. I sure didn't want to listen to that. It scared me to think we might leave him, and the ranch, and come to live in the city where there was nothing to do. I plotted my getaway to parts unknown, should that occur.

Our trips back to Seneca always passed in a blur. I probably slept for most of the way, worn out from a week of being good and trying to figure out what made those people tick.

A World of Words

It was my fault we nearly got put off the train, but since I was only four the drama of our situation went right over my head.

Mom and I had been minding our own business, as usual. We didn't make a practice of visiting with strangers, but this was never much of a problem since there were few other passengers on the first leg of our trips to Omaha.

My mother was never without a book or magazine close at hand, and the long train ride provided a rare occasion for indulging in her favorite pastime. Whether genetic or environmental, the love of words came to me early and, on this occasion, I was reading aloud from my book. Suddenly, a shadow fell across the page.

"Ma'am, may I have your ticket for this child?" the conductor asked.

"Why, she's only four, she doesn't need a ticket," Mom replied.

"No ma'am, that's not true. She's obviously at least five, because she knows how to read."

According to my mother's recollection, the argument that ensued became somewhat heated before the official gave up and left us alone. I recall none of that, but then I always become oblivious when I get my nose in a book.

Most folks read a lot in those days. Our family had a horror of being snowbound with nothing new to read, but there was little chance of it happening. We subscribed to a variety of magazines. Dad leaned toward news and sports, but we all paid attention to the Saturday Evening Post, Life, Colliers, and National Geographic. Mom had her women's magazines, and I graduated to them after outgrowing Jack and Jill and American Girl, which is when censorship entered my life. Mom skimmed each article and story in her magazines, and turned down corners of pages, to indicate what she considered age appropriate for me. I let her have her illusions but read everything cover to cover when her back was turned.

Dad's censoring took a different form. He didn't allow me to buy comic books. I didn't much care, they took only a few minutes to read and weren't much fun the second time around. There were plenty to be had at the neighbor kids' homes, and occasionally those were handed down to me. Dad permitted this, likely knowing they'd provide poor competition to the fare offered at our house, and he was right.

Mom belonged to the Book of the Month Club, so there were books stacked all over the house. I could devour two or three of them a day, if left to my own devices. We got books by mail from the Nebraska Library Commission and, with a two week limit for keeping them I generally got through my favorites more than once.

Hired men kept a stash of paperback westerns in the bunkhouse and I occasionally snagged one to read. I owned all of Zane Grey's work, so sometimes traded one of those to a hired man in exchange for his latest acquisition.

Neighbors probably read less than we did because they were card players, but there were books and magazines in the homes of all country people. Strangely, I don't recall parents of my town friends reading, nor any magazines or books in their homes, other than what kids brought from school. Whether they were less interested, or just busy with social activities that were unavailable to country folks, is hard to say.

School began with opening exercises. We recited the Pledge of Allegiance, sang a patriotic song, and then the teacher read a chapter from a book someone had brought to share. If we had been exceptionally good she might be persuaded to read one more chapter. This routine ended when we got moved upstairs for sixth, seventh, and eighth grades, and I wasn't happy about it. Beginning literature class was a fair exchange, although sixth grade wasn't into it yet. I sat fascinated while the upper classes read Evangeline, The Raven, and other classics, and looked forward to when my turn would come, but our class had some slow learners so we never got that far in our books the next year.

For some odd reason, as soon as reading books were handed out at the beginning of each year, we were forbidden to read ahead in them. I was pretty compliant as a kid, but that was tantamount to a challenge, so of course, I devoured the whole book in a week. It wasn't like getting to discuss the stories in class though, and I felt cheated. The teacher was unsympathetic, and justifiably displeased that I had read on my own, rather than attending to math problems. Reading had gotten me in trouble again, but at least this time Mom wasn't involved.

The Forbidden Pleasures of a Banned Book

The Seneca Drugstore sat on the southwest corner of Main Street, though no one ever called it Main Street. Since it was the only block in town with any businesses we just said we were going over town, up town, or down town, depending on where we started from. If I was going down town, half a block from Grandma Spencer's house, chances are I headed for the drugstore.

There were other attractions along the wide gravel street: candy selections deliciously displayed directly inside Darling's General Store and a pop cooler to the left of that, where we peered into the depths of chilled water and debated whether to choose Orange or Grape Crush, Dr. Pepper, or Cream Soda. The proprietor complained if we kept the lid open too long, so we hurriedly lifted the small glass bottle out, let it drip briefly before closing the lid, put it on the counter, and dug for a nickel. I usually drank on site because it was seven cents if you took the bottle, with the two cents to be repaid when you brought back the empty. We often scavenged around town for discarded bottles, and got enough in return to pay for our treats.

Still, for my money, the drugstore held more magic per square foot than any other building in town. I don't recall there ever being a resident pharmacist, but then there wasn't a resident doctor either. We called it the drugstore because you could buy headache remedies, bandages, liniment, hot water bottles, and athlete's foot powder there, as well as some under the counter offerings that we kids were unaware of. The only thing behind that counter that interested me and my pals were the bins of ice cream and the malt machine.

Entering the drugstore, I slid onto a tall stool, rested elbows on the counter, and debated the merits of vanilla versus strawberry cones. If I'd earned a quarter by picking up enough pop bottles, I ordered a malted milk, planning to share with a friend, because they gave you the whole container, more than most adults could put away in one sitting. The malts came with a spoon because they were too thick to sip through a straw. You climbed down off the stool, took your treasure to a small round table, and sat in a wire backed chair because you were going to be there a while, and people coming and going for shorter errands always stood, or sat, at the counter.

The building had formerly been a bank, and the vault at the back was used for storage. There are faint memories of the owner coming out of that room and handing something in a brown paper sack to some sheepish looking fellow. Liquor sales were legal by then but I reckon that men who didn't want their reputations soiled by hanging around the pool hall in broad daylight chose the more discreet path to peace of mind.

The high ceiling was made of embossed tin, and wooden floors were worn by years of foot traffic. If you sat on the floor and scooted, you likely got splinters in your backside. And yes, we did sit on the floor. In the corner, by the window, away from the counter and half hidden by the tables and racks of heating pads, rupture remedies, and feminine supplies, was a magazine rack, and the bottom two shelves contained comic books. We knew you weren't supposed to really read them, only look them over long enough to choose one to buy, but of course we did read them, cover to cover, until the owner came over to run us off, and sometimes, if the store was busy, we even traded copies when we finished the one we were reading. This wasn't much of an advantage for me because I read about double the speed of any of my co-conspirators.

I had broken the rules long before getting caught, simply by virtue of Dad's ban on comic books but, if it counts for anything, I never spent any of my own cash on one. It did feel particularly naughty to sit on the floor with kids who were familiar with the worldly ways of The Road Runner, Superman, and Lash LaRue, and it was another chance to be included in a gang of townies.

I got away with disobedience, more often than not, and Mom never did catch me reading True Story.

Perspectives

Here's how I learned to hate peppermint. Not that I was over-fond of candy in the first place. What sweets we had in the house mostly consisted of chocolate cake, my mom's favorite, and the occasional cookie. Always pie on branding day or when the hay crew was present. I got burned out on chocolate pretty early, and the lemon drops that Dad brought home from town sometimes were ok, but not something to be anticipated.

But in the winter of my seventh year I was sick with tonsillitis for a long time, so Mom spent much of that school term in town with me at Grandma's. Rheumatic fever set in, and I was put to bed and given penicillin shots daily by Mary Wiley, who later married Beulah's son Courtney. Mary's son, John, was some years younger, and had already gained membership in the village brat club. I knew his mom only by sight, but she'd evidently had some nursing experience, so Doc Walker designated her as the person in charge of the needle.

When I was well enough to have my tonsils out, we went to Omaha for the operation. I must have still been somewhat run down, because Grandma and Grandpa James' doctor prescribed two large peppermint sticks the night before surgery and a big lollipop the morning of the operation. Whatever that was about, it was a lot of candy for one who didn't like it much to start with, so the adults stood over me and made sure it was all consumed. To this day, peppermint tastes like medicine to me.

Being separated from my tonsils changed me from a picky eater to a kid with a hollow leg and more energy than my mom knew what to do with. Perhaps she and Grandma Spencer had had enough of one another's company during my illness, because for the rest of that school year Mom and I stayed upstairs at Aunt Beulah's rooming house next to the hotel. It wasn't very satisfactory for a youngster who needed room to run, and our meals of lunch meat and cheese sandwiches, or pork and beans warmed on a hot plate, weren't much to my liking.

The next fall found me boarding with the Poraths, on the south side of town. I reveled in being part of this boisterous, busy family, so different from my own, and having four other children to interact with kept me too busy to be very homesick. They kept cattle, a couple of horses, and ran a dairy. Living there felt like I had one foot in town and one in the country, though not as far in the country as I'd have preferred.

Mr. Porath stood a head, and more, above his wife and took up most of the slack in his uniform of clean bib overalls and blue chambray shirt. He surely got dirty, working all day outdoors, but I don't recall him so, any more than I remember a different mode of dress for church on Sunday. His laugh was loud and hearty, but when a transgressor needed dealt with, his voice seemed to mimic that of the fire and brimstone God we heard about in the fundamentalist church we attended on the weekends I spent in town.

The children—Carol, the oldest; Melba, my age, and two younger boys, Leland and Gaylord, never seemed afraid of their father, and I can't recall being so either, but we all tended to tiptoe around him to some extent. Now I realize he was a kindly man who hid it well. The only time I saw him touch one of his youngsters was with the razor strap, and that required a particularly offensive infraction of rules. If that seems strange, they were not much different than any other family. Spankings were administered barehanded at my home, but some kids were sent to cut their own switch, and the high school principal kept a paddle with holes drilled in it in his office.

Mrs. Porath was plump, cheerful, and motherly, in an unstylish way. Her dresses were pretty prints, which she sewed herself and covered with an apron. She wore sensible shoes with a mid-heel, and I always went to sleep to the sound of those heels clicking as she went about her never-ending chores.

Melba, although a grade behind me, was already a pal. Though Carol was older, she never bossed us, and the two boys were full of fun and tricks. As a member of that energetic household, I even began to find school tolerable. They belonged to a church that offered youth activities, so weekends when I couldn't get home weren't too bad.

Night and morning, Mrs. Porath put on an old pair of her husband's overalls and a chore coat, and went to the barn to help milk. The boys helped when old enough, but we girls were in charge of house work. One of our jobs was washing and sterilizing the milk bottles: quarts, pints, and half pints, filling them as Mr. Porath separated the milk and then putting on the flat cardboard caps. There was a precision in this, because each customer had a different standing order, which could change, relating to whether company was expected or if someone was away from home.

Mr. and Mrs. Porath were always that, to me. I'd no more have considered calling them Edmund and Mildred than I'd have addressed my folks as Joe and Wilma. All other adults in our neighborhood were known by first names: Lou and Dorothy Merz, Marjorie and Wendell Merz, Vivian and Percy Miller, Clara and Alvo Crawford, Nadeane and Dwayne Andersen, Louise and Arnold Anspach; even bachelors and spinsters: Jerry, Norma, and Ralph Van Deusen, Jim Miller, and Billy Paul. Old Billy Merz was Grandpa Merz to all of us, and was indeed Grandpa, to many of my playmates. But Mom always referred to the Poraths as Mr. and Mrs., so I followed suit.

Maybe Dad decided the expense for my board and room was unwarranted; for whatever reason, the next term I was back at Grandma Spencer's, which didn't go over well with me. It seemed lonelier than ever, and in protest I took on the persona of a spoiled brat at home. By mid-term, I'd managed to finagle a move back up the hill, where I remained through eighth grade.

I wasn't privy to many discussions between my parents after starting school, so my perception of their decision for Mom to rent rooms in town for my high school years may be skewed. I adopted the mantra common to all teens. "You don't trust me!" That may have been true and, applicable to teens of any era, would have been wise. In retrospect, I note that other country moms had all moved to town with their kids earlier on, and we were just behind the times, as we always had been in matters pertaining to social and cultural norms.

I lived out of a suitcase for all of my school years, and again in college. It amazed me, while living in a dorm, that many of my classmates had never spent a night away from home, and girls cried themselves to sleep for a month. Many of them had never sewed on a button or done a load of wash, let alone ironed a blouse. I was almost grateful then for the hard years and experience gained early in life.

For thirty odd years of my first marriage we stayed settled, but after being widowed, going back to college, taking up a career, and remarrying, while continuing to ranch part time, the suitcase life is again in play.

I've come to understand I was fortunate to experience different family dynamics in those early years. What doesn't kill us makes us stronger, and I'd need those muscles.

The Whoopee

"You kids get your wraps on and get ready to go on the route. We're taking the Whoopee tonight; it's not too cold, so you can ride in back if you want."

Mr. Porath's voice was as big as he was, so no one dallied when he barked an order. Whichever two of us had been previously designated to deliver scurried across the slippery space between picket fence and driveway, frolicking through a swirl of flakes that swirled in the yard light to vie for a spot next to the cab of the rusty old power wagon that could be heard two blocks away, and settled carefully among the wire crates containing still warm bottles of milk and cream. We knew by heart the standard orders for regular customers: a quart of milk and half pint of cream for Mrs. Anspach, two quarts of milk for the Andersons, and a pint of cream every other day for Mrs. Drake, along with her daily quart of milk.

We enjoyed the Whoopee because it was one of the few times we were allowed to ride in the back of a pickup. There was no rhyme or reason as to Mr. Porath's decision to take that rather than the car, except for times when the streets were snow covered and slick. I think maybe he just liked the hot rod sound it made, the same as we did.

I don't recall anyone ever riding in the front seat, or even asking to, no matter how cold the weather. Whenever the wheels stopped, one of us grabbed the appropriate container for that house, bailed out of the truck bed, left the milk order on the porch, placed empty bottles in their wire container, and loaded up again.

There was sort of a trick to the routine. You were supposed to hurry, but a chip in one of the empty glass bottles brought a general chewing out. It had to be inclusive, since there was no way to tell whose carelessness had caused damage, and a warning that went with the deal concerned not taking the Whoopee anymore if we couldn't be more careful. That threat was enough to keep us pretty well slowed down, but I took it to heart maybe more than the others.

My family didn't have a car for a lot of the years I lived with the Poraths, and it wasn't much of a concern for me. But if I'd been consulted about what kind of motorized vehicle my dad should buy, I'd certainly have requested a Whoopee.

At Home, Wherever Home Was

Mom instructed me to always help out and not be a bother, so I was first to volunteer whenever Mrs. Porath needed a chore done. My display of willingness didn't always sit well with the sisters, who sometimes fussed about whose turn it was to pitch in. I loved living in the midst of a boisterous family, so different from my own, and never felt like an outsider, but they were surely as relived as I was when I got to go home for a weekend and their normal routine was resumed. For one thing, Melba and Carol took turns sleeping with me in their bedroom, and the odd one slept on the living room couch. I hated this, but my requests to take a couch turn were denied, likely because the parents felt a paying boarder deserved a real bed.

Poraths were active in church, so we were always getting ready to go somewhere. There were school activities, and the kids were in 4-H. I envied them that connection with most of the other neighborhood kids, as well as my schoolmates, even when the parents nagged about keeping up record books or finishing a cooking or sewing project in time for Fair.

Fair was a foreign notion for me, and I don't think I ever attended one until after I was grown. Dad believed that extracurricular things were a waste of time that could be better spent studying or tending ranch work. It was a moot point anyway, as we didn't get our own vehicle until I was ten, and by then I had sense enough to pick my battles over social occasions.

I generally rode horseback to visit neighbor kids on summer afternoons, after helping Mom with house chores, or checking pasture for Dad. Usually, I went to Lou and Dorothy Merz's, and we kids played in the loft of their huge barn, or dug worms and dangled them from a hook on our cane poles over at Swan Lake. If they were gone to a 4-H meeting or some such, I rode the other mile to Marjorie and Wendell Merz's to visit Karen and Georgia, who were a bit younger than me. We entertained ourselves in a blowout above their barn, or looked at pictures of their favorite starlets in a movie magazine. The ladies were lovely, but movies were a once or twice a year event for me until I reached high school. Besides, my preference leaned toward Westerns, and I was more interested in pictures of Roy Rogers or Gene Autry. Unless the visit was overnight, I seldom saw their brother, Jerry, who was enough older to be out helping his dad.

I always had to be home in time to wrangle the milk cows, so if free time was limited I might ride the two miles to Miller's. Percy and Vivian had two kids, both younger than me. Marjorie and I seemed to have little in common, but managed a quiet diversion with paper dolls or a board game. Their son, Bob, usually had his nose in a book. The Millers were people of few words; somehow, conversation seemed redundant in that household, although in group situations like card parties and brandings they were vocal enough not to be considered strange.

By and large, our summer games were conducted outdoors and at full gallop. In contrast, winter entertainment was sedentary. Board games were big with Poraths, and a few childish card games were allowed, but their church frowned on movies, dancing, and playing cards, which were all not only permitted, but enjoyed, by my parents and our country neighbors. Winter pastimes at the Poraths, other than those conducted around the big oak dining table, consisted of parties for the Young People's group at church or school activities.

We preferred games to homework, around that table, but Mrs. Porath, who had been a teacher, ruled our study sessions with a velvet glove. She never raised her voice, and I never heard a word of gossip cross her lips, but reprimands for misbehavior left no doubt about lines not to be crossed. When she explained to me that "darn" was simply a substitute for "damn," I never used slang in her presence again.

Looking back, it seems surprising how seldom we were sick. I recall a few times when we were all shivering under blankets and burning with fever; my parents getting up only to tend the fire and heat up some soup, but these were rare.

Colds were doctored according to the custom of each household. Some people made a steam tent with teakettles of hot water and towels draped over the head. My mom favored store bought remedies; Vicks rubbed on the chest, covered with a flannel rag and topped with a hot water bottle. A dab of Vicks in each nostril was supposed to open a stuffy nose but I never found much relief in that method, probably because I hated the smell of it and wiped it right off. We kept Smith Brothers cough drops for a stubborn case of the croup, but I disliked that taste so usually spit them out.

Mrs. Porath mixed up a concoction of turpentine and lard to rub on the chest before applying the flannel and hot water bottle, but you had to be careful about the heat, or you ended up with blistered skin. She gave us a tablespoon of warm honey mixed with cream for coughs.

Grandma Spencer used honey too. Her cough remedy was stronger; she mixed equal parts of honey, lemon juice and whiskey. Children's dosage was one tablespoon; I don't know if adults tended to require larger amounts, but it seems quite likely. This remedy was almost worth getting sick for, and I much preferred it to cough drops, but to this day I dislike undiluted honey. It must not have been the "spoonful of sugar" that made her medicine go down so smoothly.

Music in the Air

The only recollection I have of Mrs. Porath sitting down is when she played the piano of an evening as we gathered around to sing hymns. She played beautifully, whether at home, church, or a community function, and required her daughters to sit straight backed and hold their hands level as they practiced weekly lessons. Carol kept a supply of the latest sheet music in the piano bench, so after her mother finished playing hymns she took over the keyboard and we sang whatever was popular.

My feelings about the music were mixed—a bit of envy at the other girls' expertise, and smugness because I had managed to talk my folks into stopping lessons with Mrs. Mann a few years earlier. It occurs to me now that Mrs. Porath could have given me lessons, and I might have been more receptive. It's certain that she could have used the money, and just as certain that my parents couldn't have afforded both room and board and music lessons.

Each member of the Porath family played an instrument and contributed to the church orchestra. Here was another area where I was an outsider. I often went home on weekends, so my musical contribution was singing, and I sang my heart out. That was my own family legacy. Grandma Spencer sang old favorites in her shaky soprano, as she went about her chores, and my other grandparents always listened to music on their bedside radio, so when we visited there I went to sleep hearing classical music or the Mormon Tabernacle choir from across the hall. Dad and Mom sang along with the radio, and Dad even sang or hummed when he danced. I sang at play, on horseback, and while milking the cows.

When the Merz family stopped by to visit of a summer evening we kids sat on the top rail of the corral or in the open door of the hayloft and sang to the moon, harmonizing poorly, but enthusiastically, as we belted out every song we knew: *Goodnight Irene, Your Cheating Heart,* and *Tennessee Waltz.* If we ran out of popular stuff, we reverted to old standards like *Clementine* or rounds we had been taught in school. One summer my mother forbade me to sing another note of *On Top of Old Smokey*, swearing I would surely drive her insane. I generally rode back and forth to Seneca with the Merz family on weekends, and we kids sang all the way there and back, so chances are that Dorothy wanted to stuff rags in our mouths more than once.

I stopped singing early in my first marriage, for reasons so complex they are unclear to me to this day, but I can't recall Grandma Spencer without hearing *When You and I Were Young Maggie* or *When Johnny Comes Marching Home,* in my head, and my memories of Mrs. Porath are embroidered with the click of her "sensible shoes" as she bustled around the house after the rest of us were settled in bed, and falling asleep to the soft strains of *The Old Rugged Cross.*

Regrets

I threw away the music the year I was seven. That was when I cajoled my parents into letting me stop piano lessons.

I suppose some part of me always wanted to play music. Most kids will pound on a piano if one is available, and I was no different. But piano, as such, never interested me because the music I liked best was made by guitars. Not that I knew anyone who played guitar, other than some fellows in local dance bands, but there was Roy and Gene on the radio and in movies, and those guys on the Grand Old Opry.

I somehow think it was Dad's idea for me to trudge a block and a half from Grandma Spencer's big yellow house one afternoon a week, knock on Mrs. Mann's door, and sit in her stuffy, cluttered living room on a hard piano bench, straining to make my hands reach a whole octave. Dad had always wanted to take music lessons, Mom had some degree of proficiency on the piano, and Grandma owned one, so this decision probably made sense to everyone, and may have been one of the few things they all agreed on.

Mrs. Mann's hands were crippled with arthritis, but she could still give lessons, and likely needed the money. She'd lumber across the worn carpet, sit down next to me and ask, "Did you practice this week?" I answered in the affirmative, but just how halfheartedly I had practiced would soon become apparent.

She frequently stopped me in the midst of scales to remind me to keep the backs of my hands straight, and chastised me for stopping to start over when I hit a wrong note. "Continue on," she said. "You never know; the people listening may not even hear your mistake, and you'll learn to do it right by letting the music flow along."

I disliked her sitting so close. I've always been particular about personal space, although it would be years before I learned to recognize the cause of discomfort that almost becomes panic when I'm in a tight space. Mrs. Mann was oblivious to this I'm sure, as she leaned close, squinting at the music before me, white head nodding in time as she counted aloud, "one and two and—wait, that's a rest, remember? And the C is a half note, not a quarter."

She smelled funny too. A combination of denture breath, which I recognized from my Grandma James' hugs, and what I now know was probably leakage from an aging bladder.

Obviously, there had been a Mr. Mann, but other than being told he had died, I had no sense of her family, and never saw Mrs. Mann outside her home. Not at church, in the store or post office, or even in her yard. Perhaps she was so crippled that necessities were delivered, but she never had visitors and wasn't on the list of my grandma's after supper outings.

I was supposed to practice my music for half an hour every day but it didn't happen happily, or even regularly. Perhaps Grandma wearied of nagging, or the noise got on her nerves. I never saw her play the piano, and don't know how she came to own one, and I can't say why I resented learning. There was little else to do on those long lonely evenings, so I might as well have practiced. The fact is that I did not.

I began a relentless campaign to stop the lessons, and can still hear the sorrow in Dad's voice when he gave in. "You'll be sorry someday," he said, and I am. Not only for lack of musical skills which might have helped heal the ragged edges of life, but for throwing away the gift he tried to give me, for disappointing him, and for embarking on a life-long pattern of quitting whatever seemed too troubling or inconvenient. I never mastered the art of continuing after hitting a sour note, but I have come to know that every time you quit, it gets harder to start over.

In the Land of Milk and Honey

When I was four years old my mother gave me her first piece of adult advice. "Never learn to milk the cow."

She didn't say why, and I didn't bother to ask. Being the independent soul I was, and still am, I coaxed Dad into teaching me to milk that very evening. It was harder than I expected, but being the stubborn soul I was, and still am, I persevered and eventually mastered the chore. I always enjoyed it, except on sultry summer evenings when flies made mincemeat of the cow and the milkmaid, and Bossy hadn't lifted her tail completely before relieving herself. It helps if one ties the cow's tail to her leg, but then she can't swat flies at all, and is likely to kick over the bucket.

Even on winter mornings that made me cringe at the thought of removing mittens, there was comfort in putting my head in the cow's flank. Soon enough, the warmth of hands transferred to cold teats, and squirting milk into the open mouths of barn cats was a pleasant diversion.

When Dad carried the milk pails to the house, he often swung a half full one over his head to amuse me, so I never had trouble understanding centrifugal force. After I was old enough, he let me turn the crank on the cream separator, but this was a chore that required some skill. The speed with which one turned the crank determined how thick the cream was, and Mom wanted her cream thick enough to spoon, rather than pour.

Porath's electric separator took the guess work out of that deal, but one thing remained constant; the separator must be washed. The chore fell to the unluckiest person, because it was very tedious. There were a great number of cone-shaped discs that must be washed thoroughly, individually, and daily, while being kept in order. The longer one put off the chore, the more difficult the job because cream sours quickly in warm weather. Failure to put the separator back together properly resulted in milk spurting all over the floor and the separator operator, so nobody ended up happy, least of all the person who mixed up the discs.

One aspect of having a milk cow that I didn't relish was churning butter. The churning was a chore that Mom could, and did, turn over to me at a young age. I barely recall the large wooden churn, but as soon as I was old enough to sit and turn the crank we got a smaller one; simply a gallon jar with a lid containing a handle, with paddles attached. Mom sat me on the floor and told me to turn the crank until I saw yellow chunks.

I found all manner of reasons to dislike that job, most having to do with the need to sit still. My hand was tired. It was boring. It took too long. More times than not, I'm afraid, Mom gave up because I had monkeyed around stopping and starting until the cream was too warm and had to be put back to chill again. This involved finding other jars with tight lids because opportunities for refrigeration were primitive. In summer, the jars went into a tank of water in the milk house. In winter, they were put on a windowsill outdoors, or in a snowbank.

The milk tank was an oblong affair that resided in the shack with the separator. A pipe on one end of the tank carried water in from a windmill, and another pipe at the other end drained into a stock tank in the corral. Milk, cream, butter, and other perishables were put in quart jars and floated in the tank. Crocks of pickles, sauerkraut, or meat sat on a shelf made of old mower sickles which was suspended with wires and hung about halfway from the top. Plates weighted down with bricks were used for lids. I could never undo the lids Mom had put on jars to seal out water. Sometimes, even Dad declared her "wicked twist" too much for him.

Eatingers always kept greyhounds for hunting coyotes. The dogs were usually penned until time for a hunt, but greyhounds are notorious escape artists so they often ended up at our place or that of another neighbor. After such an excursion, they were hungry or thirsty. Dad usually came up with some sort of food for them before taking them home, but on more than one occasion they helped themselves to something from the milk tank. It was no trick for them to push a plate off and devour the contents of a crock, but we never did figure how they could unscrew a jar lid and lick out the cream.

We drank skim milk at home, but Mrs. Porath kept a jar of whole milk in her refrigerator. For customers on the milk route, the separated milk went into a tapered glass bottle until the neck began to narrow, after which it was put under the cream spout until full, and then topped with a cardboard cap. When the housewife wanted whole milk for drinking, the bottle was shaken up to mix. Customers who wanted cream for other purposes ordered it by pint bottles. Each bottle was wiped clean and placed in wire crates, left on a front porch or step, and empties from the day before were placed in the crates to be taken home, washed and refilled. We kids never collected money so that must have happened when Mr. Porath did the morning delivery.

All ranch families kept a milk cow or two, as did people who lived on the edge of town and had room to pasture one. The McIntosh family lived in a tumbledown house on the far side of Seneca. There were five children at home and an invalid father. Mrs. McIntosh took in washing, which to my knowledge was the only income source besides part time jobs the kids could find. I suppose there were enough bachelors and railroad men coming and going to make it viable. My only memory of the mother is seeing her bent over the wash tub or in church on Sunday. But the family had a milk cow that was kept at Porath's, and Raymond, who was in my grade at school, rode his bike over to milk that cow and carried the milk pail home on the handlebars. I have no notion what arrangements were made for breeding or pasture keep, and business matters were never discussed in front of the kids but, knowing the Poraths, it seems likely they decided to forego

71

payment, out of Christian kindness.

John, the oldest McIntosh boy, was the first summer hay hand I had a crush on. He was probably in his early teens when he hired on as chore boy and stacker team driver, and of course, wouldn't have had a clue about the eight year old who worshipped him from afar. I recall Dad scolding John for running the milk cows in on a gallop, and you'd think if that made such a lasting impression I'd have taken it to heart and not needed the same tongue lashing a few years down the road. Apparently, that was my first encounter with the concept that love overlooks whatever spoils the notion of perfection in the object of affection.

Still, I took pride, during my teens, in having the responsibility of barn chores and wrangling horses, and even during the busy years of raising kids, helping with ranch work, and then coming in to do chores before getting supper, I enjoyed milking.

I never regretted learning to milk until many years later, when my children's father stayed late in town, or at a farm sale, knowing the chores would be done when he returned. At that point, I realized my mother possessed more wisdom than I had been willing to admit.

Bachelors

Our neighbors were just who they were. The bachelors, and we had several, had their quirks, but nobody gave those things any thought.

Billy Paul was a balding man of middle age, though he seemed old to me. "Hard of hearing," was how he described himself, and it was an understatement. He resided alone in a little shack near Lowe Lake, which is west of the Merz ranches, and didn't mingle much. I recall stopping by there once or twice with Dad on some kind of errand, and Billy showed up at some neighborhood picnics or the occasional funeral. Most of my recollections of him are when he dropped in at our place to chat on his way to or from someplace, but perhaps that's not accurate either. Maybe he really was lonely and just wanted to hear the sound of a human voice, no matter how faint.

Dad and Billy would visit, a process mostly consisting of shouted comments by Dad, punctuated by, "Hah?" or "What was that?" from Billy, in an equally intense tone. I guess he couldn't hear himself, either. Mom stayed on the sidelines, except for offering cookies and iced tea, and my impression was that Billy liked it that way. He always seemed shy around womenfolk, and if Dad was away when he happened by, Billy simply bid us good day and went along home.

I never knew of Billy having any family ties in the community, or hearing where he hailed from. Jerry Merz says that Billy just sort of disappeared from our midst, leaving no word of his intentions. He remembers my dad saying that he had looked Billy up one time, while he was traveling in Kansas. Jerry had no idea how Dad came to track him down, but said that Billy didn't seem overjoyed to have been discovered. Dad ignored that weak welcome. If you had been a friend or neighbor in the past, he considered the connection permanent.

Jim Miller never married but, unlike Billy, Jim liked social occasions and could hold up his end of conversation with the neighborhood wives. Perhaps that came of living with his widowed mother, Katie, on the home place down on Calf Creek. When Katie's health failed, she moved to Mullen to live with a daughter in law. Jim stayed on at home, but was always included in community affairs and particularly enjoyed the winter card parties. He was usually the odd man out, but sometimes a youngster was present who was at that awkward age between childhood and teens; just a tad too old to join the group making mischief in a back bedroom. That kid was partnered with Jim, who carefully explained each play and never minded getting low prize at the end of the evening. He was more patient than our parents, and taught a lot of kids to be pretty sharp Pitch players.

The few times I was in Jim's house after his mother left there were stacks of magazines and books everywhere, and dishes on all the flat surfaces, but it never seemed dirty to me. He was gone a lot, serving several terms as County Commissioner, and when someone kidded him about not having gotten better roads built to his place he just ducked his head and smiled.

Jim's weakness was farm sales, and his self-proclaimed motto was, "It may be junk when they sell it but when I get it home, it's merchandise." Frequently, he stopped by our place when my kids were small, to drop off a box of miscellaneous items from his latest outing. The youngsters didn't know scat about merchandise, but broken BB guns, a wagon with a missing wheel, or rusty harmonicas were treasures to them.

When my husband needed a part to repair a piece of our outdated machinery he went to Jim's and asked if he happened to have such-and-such lying around.

"You know, I think there's one out behind the shed," Jim would say, grabbing a shovel. Sure enough, about a foot underground, he'd unearth the requested item. Sometimes it was even in good enough shape to be used. After he died in a tractor accident, the farm sale took three days, and folks were hauling off trailer loads of "merchandise" for three weeks.

Ned Raine lived two miles east of us, on the Box T Ranch. I doubt if his house ever had seen a paintbrush, and it was in about the same shape as Clate's. I never remember being warm when we visited him. He occasionally had a hired couple living with him, and Mom made friends with the wives, likely thinking they needed some female support. She sometimes kept in touch with those ladies by mail long after they had left the community.

Ned had a thick English accent, which made him hard to understand, and he was nearly as deaf as Billy Paul but Dad admired him a lot, and they visited often. He was well educated and a very acute businessman. Nobody ever got the better of Ned in a deal, and he always knew to the penny how much money he had. He often had most of it folded up in his wallet, and according to one neighbor, who roomed with him at the Castle Hotel in Omaha during a marketing trip Ned had ten thousand dollars on him that day.

Ned tended to pay cash for items like an automobile. It's reported that once he was dickering for a new ride and asked if the vehicle would be cheaper without the radio. Well, yes, it would.

"Take it out," said Ned. "And the back seat... would it be cheaper without that?"

Affirmative.

"Take that out too, there's only one of me."

But unlike Jim and Billy, Ned had an eye for the ladies, one of whom was Suzanne Ward, who ran a café in Thedford, and often cooked with a cigarette hanging out of one corner of her mouth and hair hanging in her eyes. Maybe that was the best Ned could do, since he drove a car with no back seat or radio. I never heard whether he took out the heater too.

Moving On

People were on the move a lot in those days, looking for a job, a handout, some excitement, or a place where their names weren't known to authorities.

There was little fluctuation in our school population, or the neighborhood, other than hired men who came and went, and many of those were already known to us. Perhaps there would be a new student for half a year, but most of them were somehow related to the community. Someone had fallen on hard times and farmed a kid out to grandparents while getting back on their feet, or the whole family came to stay with kin for the duration of an illness. New teachers came occasionally but, for the most part, our world was stable, right down to the transients.

Hoboes have always been a fact of life in railroad towns, and we took them for granted. Grandma Spencer usually fed them in exchange for some little chore she assigned, but other homes turned them away. It was said that a secret code existed among those who rode the rods or hid in boxcars—some kind of identifying mark on houses which indicated the residents were good for a meal and, while unproven, it might have been true.

Grandma's house was only a block from the tracks, and that may have had to do with the frequency with which a ragged, unshaven drifter knocked at her back door. I never knew any of them to approach the front entrance, any more than I knew her to turn anyone away. If there was some odd job to be done, wood to chop, a branch needing trimmed, or snow to shovel, she set them to the task and proceeded to butter the bread. Otherwise, they waited patiently outside until she handed out whatever she had managed to cobble up. They thanked her and took off. That was that, and no more said.

I don't remember seeing any of those men loitering around

Town, or begging for money. We kids weren't to talk to them, but since we had our own mischief to be about, it was no concern for us, and our elders seemed nonchalant about strangers in our midst.

That wasn't so true out in the hills. A tramp sometimes appeared out of nowhere, and we were suspicious. With no railroad track for a dozen or more miles, and no road but a two track trail, how did they come here, and what did they want? What were they running from, and were they desperate? The women always hoped bums wouldn't appear when they were home alone.

The Gandy Dancers were a different deal. Gandy Dancer was slang for railroad workers who lived in furnished boxcars while doing track repairs. Outfits were stationed at a location for a week, or a month, depending on the amount of work needing done. Seneca had all the amenities for traveling workers—a pool hall, bar, movie house, and café.

Some mornings, word went around among the womenfolk. "Gandy train pulled in last night." We kids were warned not to play down by the tracks, to be home by dark, and not speak to strangers. The difference in concern about Gandys and hoboes was probably twofold. The Gandys were younger, and would be around for a while, with free time, and money to spend at the bar.

With that being said, I know of no one who had an encounter with those traveling laborers. In fact, I don't even recall seeing anyone on the street that had been identified as a Gandy Dancer. They mostly stayed to themselves, probably playing poker and boozing a bit in their makeshift quarters after work.

No specifics were spoken to us, but the phrase that could bring the most rebellious juvenile wanderer into line was, "Better watch out. The Gandy Dancers will get you." Apparently all cultures have their unique concept of a boogeyman.

Use it Up, Wear it Out, Make Do

All of the families I knew used whatever was at hand, and seldom bought new. Tables and chairs might be homemade or rescued from someone's attic. My dresser was made of old orange crates and many people's bookcases were too.

Pop bottles, when we got pop, which was a rare treat, were redeemed for a few pennies, and we kids roamed the streets picking up discards in order to afford some candy or gum at the general store. Gallon vinegar jugs were made of glass, and when empty, we covered them with burlap feed sacks which had gotten too holey to hold grain. They made fine water jugs for the hayfield when soaked in the horse tank to cool. When it was time to go to the field, they were retrieved and hung on the slide stacker to supply refreshment for overheated hay waddies.

Worn shoes were half soled, often at home. Dad had a cobbler's last in the shop, which I never knew him to use, but I'd bet he grew up wearing shoes repaired at home. We took our repair business to Mr. Davitt's harness shop in Seneca, where boots and shoes were fitted with full soles and heels over and over, until outgrown, or the tops wore out.

Women darned socks, patched elbows and knees, and turned collars and cuffs to get a bit more wear. Men repaired harness, tacked tin over holes in roofs and wood floors, and used oil was poured on more of those ragged gunny sacks, to make cattle rubs.

There weren't any thrift stores, probably because the notion of getting something new before the old wore out was foreign to us. But our moms made, or bought, clothing with an eye to who would be second in line when the first kid outgrew it. Many of those garments were made from flour sacks, and women involved themselves in choosing that merchandise with an eye to future sewing projects. The sacks made good dishtowels too, when hemmed, and often our dishes and silverware had been acquired one piece at a time, as premiums for buying a certain brand of detergent or cereal.

Laundry baskets were never store bought. Apples, peaches, plums, and pears were purchased in the fall, by the bushel, and the wooden baskets they came in were recycled for laundry. You could purchase an oilcloth liner made for that purpose, to keep the clothes from snagging on the inside of the baskets.

On washday, Mom enlisted Dad's help in hauling buckets of water from the windmill to fill a large copper boiler which had been placed on the coal range. The fire was kept stoked after breakfast and articles of clothing were placed in the boiler, along with powdered soap. Many women made their own soap, and it was considered better for laundry than commercial products, but my mother wasn't willing to pioneer to that point. Besides, where would we get the latest silverware or drinking cups without those premiums?

Mom used a sawed off broom handle to stir the clothes, and when the water had cooled a bit, she fished them out and wrung them by hand. An old saying was that a girl wasn't old enough to marry until she was able to wring out clothes that had come directly from the boiler. Most of them probably cheated, like Mom, who held them over the boiler with the stirring stick for a while.

The clothes were then placed in a galvanized tub of cool rinse water, which had also been hauled from the windmill. There were two rinse tubs, one containing bluing, to whiten whites and brighten colors. After the final rinse the clothes were wrung out again, and placed on bushes in the yard, with the hope that wind wouldn't carry them off before they dried.

Eventually, we acquired a wringer washer that ran on gasoline, but it had to sit outside on the porch because of the exhaust fumes. Water still had to be carried and heated in the boiler, then transferred to the washer by bucket. In the winter, when it was too cold to be outdoors, the washer sat idle while the old method was employed. During wet weather the clothes were placed on wooden racks next to the range and the house was steamy all day.

About the time we got the washing machine Dad built a clothesline, and on days that were bitter, but fair, Mom hung clothes outdoors to freeze dry. Her fingers were generally cracked and bleeding in winter. The clothes didn't always have time to freeze dry before dark, in which case they were brought in and stood up near the stove, until they thawed enough to drape over a chair, or the wooden rack. Freeze drying wasn't an ideal situation, because it weakened the fibers in garments, and made them wear out more quickly.

I loved to help hang clothes in summer, by handing items from the basket to Mom, and if I had resisted the temptation to swing on the wires or play house in the sheets, my reward was a ride back to the house in the bushel basket. I'm still convinced that the proper way to dry clothing is outdoors, probably because a basket of wet clothing is my magic carpet. There at the clothesline, in the cool of a June morning when doves and blackbirds are celebrating summer, I become five years old again.

Living in Shanty Town

I grew up in shanty town but that was no big deal, because I didn't realize it at the time. It was probably a big deal for Mom, who had enough worldly experience to compare and contrast, but Dad would barely have noticed without reminders, which Mom supplied on a regular basis.

Three claim shacks pushed together was my first home but I have no memories of a Christmas tree, of a table crowded with hay crew, of playing on that porch, or visits from neighbors or relatives there. It seems like I didn't exist until we moved, and yet, I don't remember moving either.

After the old house became a bunkhouse I loved going in there to play when the men were gone, wandering through the rooms and wondering what it would be like to live there, having my own room, a separate kitchen, and a place to keep my toys besides under the bed. That I had indeed lived there never quite seemed true, although Mom told stories of brushing snow off my crib, and being afraid I'd be bitten by rats that scurried across the floor at night. Were they really rats? I never saw one on the place, and certainly spent a lot of time in outbuildings where they would have been. Perhaps the culture shock was so great for her that mice loomed larger than usual.

The garage sat across the driveway to the west. Besides the barn, it was the sturdiest outbuilding. It wasn't large, would have held one vehicle if we had owned any, but we didn't, so it was used for storage.

The shop, north of the new house, was in even worse condition than the bunkhouse. Blue sky was visible through the roof on a good day, otherwise rain or snow poured in, making it impossible to work there. It must have been a barn or stable, at some point, because the door was two halves, and the top hung crookedly from one hinge. The bottom part sagged so much it was almost impossible to close, so we didn't. If there had ever been glass in the windows, no evidence of such remained. The floor was dirt, and there were iron piles everywhere, a forge that I loved to pump by hand, silver curls of shavings from the drill, and a cobbler's last. It was pretty primitive, but typical for the times, and the neighbor's shops didn't look much different.

Dad claimed the barn used to sit where the shop resided, and that it had blown away in a tornado when he was quite young. I don't know when the new barn went up, but that was where the most activity took place. My swing was in the first stall in the cow barn, and Dad hung sides of beef there after butchering, which had to be done in cool weather. The carcasses were wrapped in an old sheet to keep flies off. We just went out and cut off whatever was going to be dinner, but in winter it had to be sawed off and thawed before cooking. No one was concerned about freezing and thawing, and we never got sick from it. Sooner or later, Dad boned out the remainder of the meat and brought it in to be canned. Canned beef was our winter fare, along with the occasional old hen, boiled up for a batch of noodles. This meant that we never had hamburger, which is probably why I'd rather have hamburger than steak to this day. I helped scrape and salt the hides from the butchering, and other critters that died, and roll them for tanning, but what Dad did with the leather escapes me, other than cutting some rawhide for harness repair and such.

We kids played constantly in the haymow, opening the door to sit with feet dangling, building forts in the grain bins, and hiding in the loose hay that had been pitched up there every fall. I balanced precariously on the sides of stalls to check out barn swallow nests in the rafters, and hunted for new kittens in the mangers. We didn't have a chicken house then, so the hens lived in the barn too, roosting wherever, and hiding nests in odd places. There were usually late hatches of chicks, and many failed to survive the winters.

The milk house was even more rickety than the shop. It sat just east of the new house, adjacent to the corral, and housed the cream separator and the oval shaped tank which served as a refrigerator in summer. The milk house leaned decidedly to the south from years of buffeting by north winds. There was no door to shut out that wind. A cracked window on the north let in enough light to see what each jar in the tank contained. There was another shed south and east of the milk house that became a shop when the old one fell down.

Improvements happened mostly without my noticing. I don't know if the present chicken house was new, or moved in, but it was in good shape, and needed to be, because its roof became the new playhouse for me and my friends. I don't recall when it replaced the old shop, or what happened to the old garage building. Probably the changes occurred during the school year, and I was seldom home from September to May.

The cave, for storing home canned fruit and vegetables, and potatoes, which we bought in hundred pound sacks, was dug on a hillside one summer when I was home. A new bunkhouse was built when I was about ten, after the old one burned. I helped trowel the foundation for that, and learned about the propensity of cement to eat holes in bare hands. It was tile block like the house we lived in, and the two rooms and double garage went up quickly. Its sloped roof provided another play place for me and my friends, but we were not allowed there when anyone was in residence
.

Those in residence were mostly single hired men, but one winter we had a young married couple there. Perry and Dot Pearman had a small baby. Their quarters were even more cramped than ours; at least our two rooms were bigger, and we had an entry way to hang coats, and a pantry.

The few other married couples that worked for us provided their own quarters, tiny trailer houses, and one summer even a tent.

84

All of us used the outhouse, so some planning for that necessity became part of our routine.

The tent was occupied by the Cash family. "Heavy" Cash looked just like his name, and his wife, Vera, was as slender as he was fat, which caused me to recall the nursery rhyme about Jack Spratt, and his wife. They had a passel of kids, and I don't know where they all managed to sleep because the tent wasn't all that large. Heavy moved quite deliberately, but Vera worked constantly, and probably would have made the better hired hand for my dad. I perceived the family as dirty, but in retrospect they were only ragged, and often went to the horse tank to bathe after dark. Vera had even less to do with than my mom, but she did the best she could.

Having another family on site was uncomfortable. I was not to bother them, and evidently the Cash kids were likewise instructed; a huge constraint, because I was used to having the run of the ranch. I tried not to look that direction when outdoors, even though several of the kids were in my room at school, and well known to me. The men worked together but the women ignored one another, other than when they happened to meet at the windmill for water, or at the clothesline. That seems strange now, for women who no doubt longed for fellowship, and children with no other companions, but evidently there was an unspoken class distinction between degrees of poverty.

That summer, Mom acquired a three burner kerosene stove to cook on. It gave off plenty of heat too, but less than having to use the coal range. The oven was simply a metal box that sat atop two burners, which limited the space for top stove cooking, but at canning time, more stove top was required and the range got fired up again.

Menfolk could escape to the shady lawn for a rest after meals, and enjoyed a slight breeze in the hayfield, but Mom and I had to stay in that kitchen preparing for the next round, which usually involved baking. After the men left for work, Mom often stripped to her underwear, and I went to the bedroom and lay on the cool cement floor with an ear cocked to warn her if any of the crew should return for something. Sometimes we placed a blanket under a shade tree in the yard, or went to the milk house to plunge our wrists into the icy water, which cooled us for all of five minutes, but with no electric fans it was our best option.

Dad rigged a shower for the men out by the milk house, consisting of a hundred-fifty gallon barrel placed on shoulder high supports. It had boards on three sides for privacy. The barrel was filled with a hose in the morning and sun warmed the water enough to make it tolerable for showers after supper. Mom and I had to make sure to stay inside during shower time, and were confined to sponge baths. I sometimes resorted to the horse tank during afternoons when the men were gone. The rest of the year we all made do with a washtub of water which was placed next to the stove. Blankets were draped on chair backs all around it for privacy. Youngest went first, and on up the chain of command, with Dad last in line. Hot water was added as needed, but the original water wasn't changed so the last person probably didn't emerge a lot cleaner than when he got in. This was the routine at many of my friends' homes too, even in town.

About half of the town folks still had outhouses. The standard for "necessities" was loose, and varied by family. All our neighbors in the country had phones, but Dad considered it an extravagance, and his opinion must have been common, because the only town folks who had phones were Aunt Beulah's hotel, because of the railroad business, and the Avey home, necessary because Elizabeth's dad was sheriff.

The Central telephone office was in Davitt's harness repair shop on Main Street. If you needed to make a call from your home, you called "Central" to be connected to the number of the person being called. Those with no home phone went to the shop, and gave Mrs. Davitt the number. She rang it for you and stood by listening in. Everyone assumed she listened in on all calls, but surely she had better things to do. Supposedly, she would get up nights for emergency calls, but as a rule you wanted to be there before eight in the evening or the shop would be dark. They lived in the back, but their light couldn't be seen from the street so no one could know whether or not they had gone to bed.

Few could afford to talk much by long distance, so those communications were usually accomplished through the US Mail. Mom was brought up with phone service, and sorely missed it, so when we went to town she usually stopped at Davitt's to call her parents in Omaha. I can still hear her giving the number. "Walnut 3050 please, and reverse the charges."

The cost for a long distance call increased after three minutes, and Mrs. Davitt would signal when time was up. Even though Grandpa James worked for Northwestern Bell Telephone Company and could afford the cost, he believed in keeping calls to a minimum. Between that, and Mrs. Davitt standing by, Mom's visits couldn't have been very satisfying, but for her lifetime she always had the notion that three minutes was about as long as anyone should talk on the phone.

Relatively Rich

I'm not sure if we were really poor. Despite the lack of material goods, we never went hungry. Some neighbors enjoyed indoor plumbing and wind chargers to provide electricity. Mom envied those conveniences, but I barely noticed. The criteria that made them well off in my eyes involved having siblings, or a room of one's own. Still, the roof over our two rooms didn't leak, and there was never a Christmas without presents under the tree.

Sometimes I felt ashamed for being so rich. My friends wore homemade garments or hand-me-downs. Mom didn't sew, so mine came from mail order catalogs, unless I inherited something from a neighbor with no younger sister. As an only child, I sometimes got several birthday presents, whereas my friends were lucky to get one. I even begged my mom for one single gift so I wouldn't need to hang my head when asked what I got for my birthday.

The only time I felt poor was when my parents shouted at one another while I cowered under covers or crouched outside a window, listening for the dreaded D word, wondering when it would happen, what would happen to me, and longing for a sibling to cling to, an ally against big words and a big world I had barely begun to understand, and never wanted to.

The thing I always understood was that there wasn't room for me; certainly not at home, in the two cramped rooms, where our daily routines were observed. My narrow bed took up a corner in the sleeping space and a makeshift dresser for my things stood behind the door. A tiny closet held my parents' clothing, and a few of my good dresses were in a box under the bed.

Toys were kept under Mom's desk in the front room, and I played there, or under the table, in order to be out from underfoot. Cement floors covered with linoleum were cold in winter, so I arranged marbles or played jacks on the old bearskin rug, or simply lay in a pool of sunshine stroking the fur and pretending to be the "Snow Queen." The sleeping room was never heated, and in winter we even dressed in the front room, as soon as Dad had the fire going. Small wonder that in summer I spent every spare moment outdoors; in the barn, on rooftops, or under the woodpile, where I had a cave of sorts and kept marbles, toy trucks, bits of colored glass, or trinkets scavenged from the junk heap on the hill.

There was room for me at Grandma Spencer's house during the school year. Too much room, I thought—no place to hide from the lost feeling of not knowing how to fill up emptiness inside me. There was room for me in the classroom: my own desk, a hook to hang my coat on, and books that didn't have to be sent back to the library, but no room for me at recess, among children who knew everyone's names and games. I couldn't seem to find where to fit, a balance between being crowded out or ignored.

I tended to play in small secluded spots: behind Grandma's piano, under the library table, or in her linen closet. I wasn't necessarily out of sight, but from these hideaways I could view the world going on without me and decide whether to come out and join in; always searching for, but never finding, a place that was just my size. In some sense, I believe I'm still looking.

The Garage Wasn't Exactly Empty

There were bats in the garage. We knew this, but it wasn't the reason we seldom went inside. There was very little cause to enter a garage which contained no automobile. Had we never had a car, I wondered? No, my mother assured me, not in my lifetime. There was mention of something called a coupe, but that made no sense. To me a coop was the little triangle shaped house where we put setting hens to keep them separate from the laying flock. Queries about the confusion unearthed the information that a coupe was some sort of car my dad had owned before marrying, but my automotive background was limited, to say the least, so I felt no need to create mental images of something that had no place in our lives.

I don't recall conversations about a car, wanting one, or the inconvenience of not having one. Those surely occurred, but not during the wartime years when both gasoline and tires were in short supply. So it was natural to ignore the small red building that sat across the driveway that no one drove on.

We kept chicken feed in the garage. I recall Dad going in about sundown on some evenings, and bats flying out into the dusk. Bats were no big deal. We saw them often at that time of day, and there would be the occasional one hanging upside down in the rafters of the barn when I went there of an afternoon to play on the swing Dad had hung there.

I never went in the garage alone, but bats had nothing to do with that. The latch was a piece of oak sweep tooth that lay horizontally across the door in an iron holder. It was too heavy for me to mess with, considering that there was nothing of interest inside, other than bats, and they'd come out at dusk anyway, through a broken window pane.

The garage was torn down sometime before I reached the

age of ten. That year, Dad came driving into the yard in the fall, after selling steers in Omaha, in a shiny maroon Chevy. Did Mom know he was going to buy a car? Had they discussed it? Knowing my dad, I doubt it, but now I wish I'd asked if she was as surprised as I was. She was more appreciative, for sure, because at that point I still became nauseous at the mere smell of the inside of an automobile. Travel wasn't my favorite pastime.

I learned to drive in that car, which we kept only a couple of years before trading it off. They must have been years of good cattle prices, because Dad surely wasn't one to give up on something that hadn't worn out.

A driver's license could be obtained at age sixteen, and by the time I reached that ripe old age, I was a pro. The only question I recall of the first driver's test I took at the Thedford Courthouse was, "How long have you been driving?"

Sort of silly, I thought at the time, but having been taught to be truthful, I put down six years. The examiner didn't bat an eye, nor did he report my parents for harboring a delinquent. It didn't occur to me to notice if he hid a smile.

At Least it's Clean

Mom never quoted the mantra about cleanliness being next to godliness, but she surely believed it. Our circumstances, like most of the folks around us, were modest at best, but when Mom got discouraged at the dilapidated surroundings or tattered clothing, she'd comment, "Well, at least it's clean."

She scrubbed the worn linoleum so often that the pattern wore off. Scrubbing meant on hands and knees, and happened at least daily. Mops were for spills, in her opinion, but I don't think we ever owned one. When something spilled, she mopped the whole floor. When it was time to wash windows, curtains came down too, to be laundered, starched, ironed, and mended before re-hanging. Soapy water from dishes or the wash was poured on the front step and swept off.

Mom's method for cleaning the old house, which had become the bunkhouse, was somewhat different. The rooms all sloped in different directions. There must have been something of a foundation under them, because families of skunks often dwelt there, sometimes making it unfit for human habitation. The old floorboards were tongue and groove, but years of heavy boot traffic had worn them smooth, although in some places a nail poked up enough to catch on whatever trespassed in its space. Some boards were splintered and split, making cracks that allowed air and insects to enter. Mom scrubbed that floor with a broom. We did the weekly wash in the kitchen of that house, and when the last load had been put through the wringer the tub was emptied by buckets. Soapy, warm, water that had been boiling when poured in, was dumped on the floor and swept through the cracks.

I never knew anyone who had bedbugs, though since it was considered a badge of slovenly housekeeping to have them, no one would have been likely to advertise the fact. But Mom had a horror of getting them and was vigilant, especially in the bunkhouse. This was likely wise, given the way hired men drifted from place to place in those days, and the lack of opportunity, and often the inclination, for them to bathe.

The bunkhouse bedding was changed weekly; mattresses were pulled off and springs were painted with kerosene. I don't know if this was commonly done on other ranches, whether it was a trick learned from neighbor women, advice from her mother in law, or one of Dad's concoctions, but it worked.

Those bunkhouse beds were a half step above a bedroll on the prairie, but a tent or dugout might have been more effective at keeping out the elements. Numerous holes in the roof got patched, but cracks of light showed through the walls or ceiling in most of the rooms.

A coal range in the kitchen was the only source of heat. There was a sink and a hand pump for washing up. A cracked and cloudy mirror hung above it, along with a rack to hold rough hand towels, and a holder for Lava soap.

The other rooms held a variety of army cots and old iron bedsteads with sway backed springs. Army blankets and old quilts, ragged from years of use and many launderings, were laid three or four deep above frayed sheets passed down from the boss's beds. But the beds were clean, and as comfortable as Mom could make them. Each was topped with a bedspread, also worn and faded, but a silent tribute that even a drunken drifter deserves a memory prompt of home and better times.

Not all the fellows who resided in our bunkhouse fell into the drifter category. For one thing, the worst choices Dad made, whether out of desperation for an extra pair of hands, or simply bad judgment, didn't last long. There was the occasional bum who sneaked into the kitchen and drank vanilla, or swigged his bunkmate's hair tonic, but they were swiftly dealt with. A few unwashed souls probably should have been run through the dipping vat along with the cattle. Dad, or Clate, would tell this genre to gather their gear after supper and then drop them off at the pool hall in town, but there was no guarantee they wouldn't come home with a replacement of the same ilk.

Haying help brought a bit more variety and excitement. It took half a dozen extras to put up hay, and this was true for both horses and men. Teams used on hay equipment had been turned out all winter and were half wild. I enjoyed watching the rodeos that took place during the first harnessing, and the runaways that happened when horses discovered they were being chased by a pile of chattering iron and a cursing hay waddie. The fellows were often high school boys, green, but teachable, and pretty apt to return to work on Monday morning, unlike some of winter's leftover crew.

In winter, we, and all the neighbors, generally kept one hired hand, so it didn't matter at whose table I sat, the hired man's face was well known to me, often a local bachelor, Jerry or Ralph Van Deusen, whose home was whichever bunkhouse where the bedroll got stashed, or someone like Milt Crawford, whose powerful thirst could be controlled for a time by staying sequestered miles from temptation. These were generally married to some goodhearted woman who kept food on the family table in town by teaching school, giving music lessons, or working at The Beanery. She kept a tight hold on her earnings, knowing that when the man got back to town his paycheck would end up in the hands of the barkeep. The fellows just played musical bunkhouses. They usually had a car of sorts, and went to town on Saturday night or when the last good time had worn off.

Dad never liked to pay his help all the wages they had coming, on the theory that they'd be more likely to reappear if they were still owed money. Sometimes it worked, but it was always up for grabs whether they'd reappear on Monday or celebrate longer, and require till Wednesday for recovery. After this happened several times in a row, they would be handed their time, whereupon they went to town, stayed drunk for a couple of weeks, and then hired on at the ranch down the road. By then, the neighbor's hired man had followed a similar pattern and was filling the vacancy in our bunkhouse. This went on for years. Employers and employees understood the game and there were no hard feelings on either side.

Fellows who had no transportation stayed put on weekends until things got unbearably dry, but we always took them along on neighborhood picnics and Sunday fishing trips, or to winter card parties. The women did laundry and ironing for them, along with that of the family, and they often reciprocated by helping with dishes or weeding the garden. In later years, I even had one who brought a bag of sugar with him because he liked his iced tea sweet and didn't want to be chastised when his glass still contained an inch of sugar at the end of a meal. When they drew their wages and asked to be taken to town they would be replaced, knowing that, in a matter of months, their feet would be under our table again.

By the time I had graduated to the status of cook, the bunkhouse was a bit more weatherproof, but still nothing fancy. I followed my mother's mantra of keeping it clean though, and the only complaint I can recall happened on Mom's watch. One morning at breakfast, shortly after the new bunkhouse/garage was built, we noticed the car sitting outside. Dad had been to a Masonic meeting the night before, and swore he had put it away. But the mystery was solved when the hired man came to breakfast.

"You must have hit a skunk on the way home last night, Joe. I couldn't take the smell coming through the walls so I got up and moved your car outside."

Dad had a habit of trying to hit any skunk that appeared on the roadway, and his aim was pretty good, so he had to own up that it was no accident, and it took Mom quite a lot of elbow grease to get that bunkhouse livable again.

The year after the old bunkhouse burned, Dad plowed the spot and planted our garden there. Like a Phoenix rising, crops stretched tall and strong, especially the strawberries. We had always had a garden, but previously, our harvesting involved a tramp across the creek and a swamp. I hated getting my Keds wet and how the mud oozed into my socks. Mom did too, so the garden had pretty much been Dad's deal.

That season was different in several ways, not the least of which was that weeding and tending became my chore. I knelt in the dusty soil, still well mixed with ashes that clung to my jeans and left an acid, gritty film on my fingers. Occasionally, remnants of melted glass or charred lumber surfaced, bruising my knees or cutting a finger, but I was fascinated by each relic, stopping to wonder what it had been before the flames altered it. What I recall most about that summer is picking strawberries the size of teaspoons, popping them whole into my mouth, savoring the juice, the red stain on my fingers, even the taste of ash that sometimes accompanied my indulgence.

We weren't concerned with hazardous waste or environmental impact statements. Surely there were old paint cans, fly spray, and all manner of cast off chemicals in the blaze that resulted from a faulty chimney on a warm October day when Dad saw the smoke from a far pasture and galloped home. We experienced no health issues from years of gardening among the ruins of the house which was Mom's first home on the ranch, where Grandma Spencer had fed a passel of kids and hired men, and where Dad and Clate had batched until they both married. The only long term damage was my mother's lifelong fear of fire, which I inherited, in spite of not having witnessed the flames, and peaceful reveries in the strawberry patch.

Time Out

Of all the moms I knew growing up, mine is the only one I ever saw sitting down to rest. None of my friends' moms seemed to be readers, but mine read even while cooking, or at meals, if it was only the two of us at home. She taught me the bad habit of reading in bed, which has cost me many a short night's rest. Mom sat down to read in the evening, or of an afternoon, when other moms would have been gardening or doing handwork. She made no excuses for her reading addiction, and I haven't either.

All my friends' moms had several kids, and even with chores assigned to each according to age, there was always more work to do than day to do it in. My mom was plenty busy, but she found time to read to me. As far as I knew, none of the other moms did that, and I didn't hear any bedtime stories when visiting at the homes of friends.

Their mothers had different ways of taking time out. Mrs. Porath sat at the piano and accompanied her kids on the various instruments they played in the church orchestra. She sat at the sewing machine, but that couldn't have been very restful, because it was generally mending, or teaching one of her girls how to make a garment. Maybe the most rest she ever got was sitting on the piano bench when she played for church or at the dining room table on Saturday night to drill us on memory verses for Sunday-School.

Donaldine Avey had her garden. It was a necessity, of course; her family would have starved without it, but she truly enjoyed growing things. I never did see her sit down except at meals.

Dorothy and Marjorie Merz and Vivian Miller sat briefly to eat, jumping up frequently to refill coffee cups or pass dessert, but they lingered long at table to visit when company came, or at community gatherings. In contrast, my mom was always first to rise and start clearing dishes, even before everyone had finished. It seemed just when conversation was getting interesting she interrupted it and made us all feel guilty for sitting when there was work to be done. But maybe that was simply her way of making more time to steal in the afternoon to read her favorite magazine.

No one else I knew ever went on vacation, but I suppose the trips to Omaha that Mom and I took probably qualified as such, in the eyes of our neighbors. When I was five, Mom, Grandma James, and I went by train to Florida to visit Mom's brother and sister-in-law, and Mom and her parents took me to the Black Hills when I was seven. None of my friends had ever been out of Nebraska, or expected to be. My parents took me to Yellowstone when I was ten, but the park was a sidelight to visiting the Wyoming relatives. I confess to having enjoyed the relatives more than the scenery, but being shut in a car with two people who disagree on almost everything is distracting, at the least. After that, we stayed put, perhaps because repeating an unpleasant experiment would have qualified as insanity.

On the whole, most women of my acquaintance scurried and stirred and scrubbed. It was what you did when you were a grown woman, and no one thought twice about the men sitting long with their coffee and cigarettes or sprawled on the lawn for an after dinner snooze.

Busy as the women were, I never heard one complain of weariness, though they had to have been nearly dead on their feet. Early examples are deeply ingrained. To this day, I have trouble sitting still, and the third day of vacation finds me wondering what all has piled up at home in my absence.

Adventures at the Merz Mansion

No one ever sat on the horsehair sofa in Lou and Dorothy's living room if they could help it. We weren't forbidden, but even the adults avoided it because it was uncomfortable enough to have adorned the waiting room in Hades, and surely a proper preparation for the tortures that lie behind that inner door.

I don't know how old the monstrosity was, or whether such an article had once signified certain social status, but there's no mystery why it lasted so well. Still, someone had used it, if only for want of a better perch. The varnish on its arms was worn off, and the leather seat showed scuffs and scratches. It was black, with a straight back that didn't go high enough to support the shoulders, and harder than a church pew. We kids used it for a slippery slide sometimes, when it was too rainy to play outdoors and too cold to play in the barn, which was even more spacious and elaborate than their house.

I was impressed with the house that old Billy Merz had built to shelter his large family, but it's likely that Dorothy would have appreciated something smaller and easier to clean. The upstairs had six bedrooms. One, at the top of the stairs, was called the sewing room, but it was where we played most, and I don't recall a sewing machine. The hallway opened out onto a balcony with a rickety railing, where we weren't supposed to play, but often did. No one seemed concerned enough to chastise us for it.

This was the only house I knew of with two bathrooms. We had none, and many of my town friends also made do with outhouses. Never mind that Merzes were as likely as not to find a snake in the tub or toilet; a bathroom is a bathroom, and you can't discount the prestige in having two.

Two downstairs bedrooms were occupied by Lou and Dorothy, and Grandpa Merz. Upstairs was the kids' domain, often shared with a hired girl, hired men, or visitors. Dorothy occasionally hosted slumber parties for a gaggle of girls, and her solution to our determination not to slumber was to set an alarm and make us change beds every hour. We drew straws for our accommodations, and the short one got the booby bed, which was the tub in the upstairs bathroom. Grandpa Merz was gone by then, and I imagine that Lou and Larry disappeared to the bunkhouse in order to avoid the ruckus, but we were too silly to notice.

I have a dim recollection of Anna Merz, Lou and Wendell's mother, who, I believe had Parkinson's. No doubt the sofa had been hers. A table, and some other pieces of furniture, carried legends of coming west in a wagon, but the most fascinating thing in the house for me was a wind up Victrola, as tall as myself. We kids played the few records that went with it over and over, letting the speed die down to a drawl and then winding it up fast. If it drove the adults crazy, no one ever told us to stop.

Dorothy was the most patient mom I ever knew, perhaps because she had no time to bother with us much. I believe she'd been hired as caretaker for Mrs. Merz, and later married into the family, continuing in caretaker role until her mother-in-law's death, which occurred when I was pretty small. By that time, Dorothy had a big yard and garden to tend, hired hands to feed, two children with developmental disabilities, and a toddler.

Billy Merz lived on into my teen years; legendary for the rhubarb wine he brewed in the basement, along with other such concoctions. He was his own best customer, but often drove his decrepit Dodge to Seneca to peddle his wares among friends.

Likely as not, he got stuck in the trail road coming or going, if not both. Granted, the road was a challenge to the best of drivers, which Grandpa Merz was not, but he'd probably imbibed enough to impair his limited abilities, and sometimes just pulled over for a nap. Or not. You wanted to look sharp when topping a hill, for a rusty maroon automobile which might, or might not, be moving, but would surely be taking its half of the road out of the middle.

The Merz mansion, which was how I thought of it, had a veranda on two sides, which made a perfect play place on rainy days or when it was too hot in the hayloft. There was an assortment of cast off furniture out there and it didn't take much imagination to conjure up games and stories. If we grew bored with exploring the nooks and crannies of the house and barn, we could choose from a plethora of old sheds and junk piles, but one of our favorite hideouts was beneath a thicket of mulberry bushes behind the house. For a while every summer our clothes and hands and faces were stained with the evidence of overindulgence, but enough berries always seemed to remain to supply Dorothy with plenty of jelly and mulberry wine.

Grandpa Merz didn't have a corner on fermentation. Many housewives of that era conjured up a mite of something celebratory. Dorothy was just a bit more adventurous. Her specialty was beet wine, and she brought it out on the least provocation.

Lou was a quiet man with a laid back manner and droll sense of humor. He loved to tell us yarns, and the one that stays in my mind concerned a tornado which had hit their place, and ours, some years before we were born. According to Lou, it did little damage, but the strange thing was that his ornery old rooster disappeared. When the dust settled, lo and behold, the rooster was in a vinegar jug atop the barn roof, with only his head sticking out. Lou broke the jug to free the rooster, which from that day forward was unaccountably docile. We didn't think to question the veracity of that tale for some years, and requested it often. He managed to tell it every time without the slightest hint of a smile. My own children, and their compadres, heard the same story and were every bit as gullible.

Lou and Dorothy put a good face on difficult circumstances; living with an invalid and a stubborn German patriarch. Grandpa Merz wouldn't have been one to let his sons carry on the ranch without intervention, and though I never heard a word of complaint from Dorothy, it was generally known that her situation was not easy. Buying a house in Seneca for sending the kids to school must have been a relief. She was an extrovert who loved visiting and composing poems and skits for community and school functions. Like as not, she viewed giving up an extra bathroom for one with no snakes as coming up in the world. The old horsehair sofa disappeared from the ranch about the same time, and no one even seemed to miss it.

Rain, Snow, or Dark of Night... Sometimes

Mom tended to check up on things. It made her feel better, I guess, to ask if the men would be late for dinner, even though for them to be on time was so rare as to find her scurrying to hurry the meal. She liked to know where I was going when I left on horseback to roam the hills, or meander in the meadow. I learned early to make up an answer, despite seldom having any notion of where I was headed or when I'd return. When we finally got a phone she was in seventh heaven, because that made it possible to track the mailman.

"Thank you for calling Montgomery Ward Customer Service. How can I help you?"

"This is Mrs. Joe Spencer at Seneca, Nebraska, and I'm checking on an order that seems to be delayed." (Mom was Mrs. Joe for most of her adult life. She never signed a check any other way until long after Dad died.) *"I expected the shipment earlier. We only get mail two days a week so it may be at the local post office, but I just wanted to check..."*

"Oh, Ma'am, you must be mistaken. There's no place in the U.S. that doesn't have daily mail delivery."

Click! Her curiosity unsatisfied; at least she had sense enough not to argue with idiots.

You couldn't really blame Mom. Getting the mail was a big deal. Most Tuesdays and Fridays, Hank Crawford's ancient Jeep negotiated a two track trail that snaked through boggy meadows, down prairie dog flats, and over sandy hills on the route that meandered north from Seneca, curved past our place, and then made a lopsided circle past Duck Lake and through miles of desolation before returning to home base.

Twice weekly was just an estimate, dependent on weather and road conditions. In winter, the main trail was often blocked with drifts, so the "snow road" wound across high spots in pastures and involved opening numerous gates. Hank wasn't young, although probably not as elderly as my child mind made him. A droughty summer meant blow sand axle deep on hillsides, and a heavy rainfall made low spots impassable, so the route involved considerable physical exertion. Sometimes our mail piled up in the post office for a couple of weeks.

If Hank made it halfway and decided, after digging out several times, that he needed to turn around and head back before dark, he often left mail for several families at the last stop. Someone at the Merz place might call Miller's to say, "Your mail is here." If the feeding was caught up and the wind was down, someone drove over to retrieve it. Occasionally, the Miller and Spencer mail just stayed where it was until Hank made his next run; disappointing, when one is snowed in, but nothing to lose sleep over.

Before we got a phone it was anyone's guess where our mail ended up. A neighbor might bring it, or sometimes Dad tied a gunny sack on his saddle and rode around the neighborhood to trace the mail. If it turned out that Hank hadn't even left Seneca, at least Dad had a good visit.

Barring getting stuck, breaking down, or having to stop at a windmill to get water for his overheated Jeep, Hank was pretty dependable in terms of arrival during good weather. In summer, I took up a vigil by the mailbox about half an hour earlier than he was due. Somehow, collecting the mail seemed like a high priority chore. When I brought it in, Mom stopped what she was doing to read her weekly letter from home before sorting her magazines from Dad's and putting the newspapers in order by date.

Having a fresh stash of reading material was almost as

good as Christmas, but in winter we were sometimes forced to start over on last month's supply. Three-day-old, even two-week-old newspapers are better than no news. We read them all, no matter how late they came. In truth, we probably all had an inherent need to check things out, but it was easier to attribute that characteristic to Mom than own it ourselves.

Mail day was such a big deal because we didn't get out and about much. Those years when the only motorized transportation was the shared pickup, it never seemed to be at whatever location was convenient.

If Mom considered our living quarters inadequate, she must have been grateful not to have landed where her sister-in-law did. The house at the Treat place—called that after the first owners— had never seen paint. The roof required Leona to have plenty of pots and pans handy when it rained, and wind rattled the windows enough to let snow sift in. A lean-to, which leaned considerably, served as shelter for a milk cow or horses, but the main herds were at our place where corrals were available. Clate's place was mostly a line camp.

Leona went into labor with her second child, Betty, on a crisp November night when the pickup was in my dad's possession, so Clate had to saddle old Casey and ride to Pearman's to borrow transportation, load his wife and one year old Sally, and drive the sandy road to Seneca.

Casey, a rangy bay, was notoriously hard to catch, but that night he allowed himself to be bridled immediately and the family made it to Grandma Spencer's before Betty arrived.

Dad and Clate were back and forth a lot, but the women and kids stayed home. Mostly, we worked, which suited me, but likely drove Mom up the wall. We had a two wheeled cart that was used for fencing and checking windmills, and a few times Dad hitched up the team and drove us to visit Merz's or Miller's. If we rode horseback for those visits in winter, my feet and hands got so numb I got off and walked half the way. Mom went reluctantly, but was probably so stir crazy she took a chance on it.

I don't remember being in Brownlee until I was in high school, though it was closer. The road was even worse there than the one to Seneca, where all our needs could be met anyway.

We went to the Mullen rodeo on the Fourth of July, and for at least the one circus, as well as for an occasional movie, after we got a car, and the theater in Seneca closed, but hardly ever to Thedford, so when I changed schools and went there for my last two school years it seemed very far away.

Prom was a whole other affair in those days. In Seneca High, the banquet was cooked by junior class mothers and served by selected sophomores in the decorated typing room at school. The dance was public; with only a couple dozen students it wouldn't have been much of an event, if closed. I don't remember any of the Junior or Senior girls wearing a formal, and Lord knows how any of the parents could have afforded one.

In Thedford, things were a bit more structured. The dance was still public, after all, the school was only a bit larger, but girls wore formals and boys at least a white shirt and tie. Mothers still cooked, and the meal was in the decorated gym, with an inspirational speaker for entertainment. Generally this was a faculty member or community leader.

Mom took me to North Platte to shop for a prom dress, all lavender lace, and strapless, with a little jacket for cover. Needless to say, I was instructed to wear the jacket. I'm not sure why we didn't just order it from Montgomery Ward, unless Mom feared it would end up at the neighbors and not reach us in time for the big day. I wore that dress again at the senior prom, as did all the other girls in my class. One formal was considered plenty, in those days, to see us though high school and any special dances in our college years. I wasn't part of the crowd that attended such occasions in college, so the high school venue was the extent of my party dress needs. It seemed to me an awful waste of money for something that went out in public only two times, and my opinion on that matter hasn't changed.

Winter in Town

It's a long time until Christmas, or so it seems to my seven year old self. At Christmas, I'll be home at the ranch but, for now, there's this day to get through.

Every morning, I get up in Grandma's chilly north bedroom and shiver while pulling on long underwear, undershirt, and long brown stockings over the underwear, fastening them to a cumbersome garter belt. The underwear stays lumpy, and I wish I was a boy and could wear pants instead of silly girl clothes. I button a plaid flannel shirt, and cover it with a corduroy jumper. After a breakfast of boiled egg, scorched toast, and weak Ovaltine, I don snow pants, coat, hat and mittens, and trudge the half block to school.

I don't like school. I mean, school is okay, I guess. It's easy for me, except for arithmetic. I like the stories in our reader, and I like my teacher. I don't like the kids, except for a few like Elizabeth and Melba, but it's good to be busy so I don't think about the ranch so much. I hate recess. They play games I'm not good at and swing too high, which scares me. And I'm always the last when they choose up sides.

School is better than after school, though. There's nothing to do at Grandma's except color or read, and I don't have many books. Saturdays are the most lonesome. If it's Sunday we walk a half block to church in the evening. There aren't any kids there, just Mrs. Beals, Mrs. Posten, and some other old ladies. Church is boring, and sort of sad, and it's always cold, because the stove at the back doesn't have time to warm the whole church before we are done. We leave our coats on, and stand to sing hymns. Even though I'm bored, I'm glad when we go; it's something to do.

School is a little better now because we are practicing for the Christmas program. I have a part to learn, and Grandma helps me with it after supper. We don't have lessons as much, because two times a day we tramp down to the hall on Main Street to practice our play and sing about Santa coming to town. But the hall is cold, too; everyplace is, except at the ranch in front of the stove.

I wonder if my mother will be at the program. I know Dad won't, but most other dads aren't coming either. It all depends on if Mom can catch a ride to town, and the weather, of course.

Mom warned me not to talk about Santa not being real so the other kids won't be disappointed. I feel kind of left out when they talk about him, like I was cheated by not getting to believe in that fairy tale. But it's no big deal, because nobody talks much about Santa, or presents. We all know not to expect a lot, even from Santa. Still, it seems a long time till Christmas. Time sure drags when I'm cold.

***

I'm glad the program is over. I remembered my lines. Mom did get to come, and now we are at the ranch. I've been helping Mom wrap presents in our cold bedroom during these short afternoons.

This morning, Dad and I climbed the hill back of the barn and he cut a branch off one of the pine trees he planted long before I was born. We brought it to the house, put it in a bucket of gravel, and stood it in a corner by the east window. I sort of wished we could have a real tree, like the one at Grandma Spencer's, with electric bubble lights, but I don't want to hurt Dad's feelings so I don't say it. I do beg Mom to put candles on ours, but she's horrified at that thought. I don't see why, it looks perfectly lovely the way they do it in my book about the night before Christmas. But that book has Santa pictures and flying reindeer, and all, so it's a fairy tale, and the candle idea must be, too.

Still, putting the flat side of our branch against the wall helped it look more like a whole tree and by the time we added paper chains, popcorn, and the plastic birds and reindeer, it looked almost fine. I pretended that the angel hair that Mom put around the bucket was snow.

Dad and I are coming in from the barn now, carrying pails of steaming, frothy milk. I stare into the twilight sky, straining to see a star and wonder if it's the one that hung over Bethlehem. It's cold enough out here to see our breath, but somehow feels warmer than all the buildings in town.

***

If I had thought it a long time till Christmas, that was nothing compared to when school would be out for summer. There were no spring breaks, not even for Easter. My bout with rheumatic fever made the days drag, even though Mom was in town with me and bringing me daily chocolate malts to make up for penicillin shots. The teacher in my mother made sure I kept up with school work, which seemed unfair. Doesn't sick mean time off?

When we moved to stay at Aunt Beulah's after my tonsillectomy, we fought about my struggle with cursive writing. Those days of isolation must have been as long and boring for Mom as for me, and she distracted us both by reading aloud John Steinbeck's *The Red Pony*, which remains a favorite book to this day.

The picture I see of myself from those days is of a sickly, sad, and solitary misfit, scared to speak, have opinions, play, or do anything that required me to come out of hiding. In summer, I blossomed into some semblance of a normal child, but each winter I climbed into my shell and waited out the cold, hoping to survive till another season of sun, but not at all convinced I would. It's unlikely that most adults who suffer from seasonal affective disorder can trace the source, but my incubation period is absolutely beyond doubt.

Small Town Christmas

A single string of colored lights at each end of the block-long main street was Seneca's sole concession to the Christmas season. A few tinsel garlands or paper chains in a shop window, a red coaster wagon with a big bow on the handle in the hardware store, and an evergreen wreath on the door of the harness shop, were the only other clues that the holidays were approaching.

Most houses had Christmas trees in living room windows, decorated with bubble lights and angel hair, but everyone knew that the packages underneath probably contained warm shirts, pajamas, or maybe stocking caps and mittens. Residents of my hometown were practical, and poor to boot, although poverty was common enough not to be remarked upon. If we couldn't afford fancy there was a bit of comfort in knowing our neighbors couldn't either.

None of this really mattered to the younger set. The focus of Christmas was pretty decorations and a variation in routine: classes abbreviated so as to practice for the school program, singing about reindeer on the roof and a babe in a manger, learning simple recitations, and drawing names at school for a gift exchange.

You weren't supposed to tell whose name you got but, of course, we did, and managed to swap slips of paper until we acquired one with the name of a best friend or secret crush. There was a two dollar spending limit on exchange gifts, and even that was a stretch for some families, especially those with several children in school. Finding a gift for teacher was left to moms, and teacher, in turn, devoted art classes to the making of gifts for us to give our parents.

After moving to Porath's, all this flurry and fuss was enhanced by rehearsals for the Sunday-School program. I'm pretty

112

sure the Sunday-School Superintendent didn't quite know what to do with me, since I was not regularly present on Sundays, and might not be there for the program unless it happened before the holiday vacation began. On the other hand, they didn't want to leave me out. I can't recall any part that I had to learn, but it was likely a very small one that would not be missed if omitted. Still, I lived in terror of confusing my lines and reciting the school piece for church, or vice-versa.

But what we looked forward to the most was a two week hiatus from school. For me it meant being on the ranch. Those blessed hours of solitude with only parents, animals, and possibly a hired man, were a respite from trying to be someone I wasn't in order to please teachers and be included in the doings of classmates.

Christmas dinner was always at Grandma Spencer's. The sturdy oak table was pushed against the wall most of the time, but at holidays was pulled to the center of the room, and leaves were added until it stretched almost to the kitchen door. Grandma spread her good lace cloth on it, almost reverently, as aunts and daughters-in-law took down good china from a narrow sideboard built into the kitchen wall and began counting out silverware.

None of this ritual mattered to me and my cousins, because we knew we would be eating at the small table in the kitchen. Being left to our own devices without stern adults chastising us about manners was fine, but what pleasured us most, at the moment, was the opportunity to create a race track around the dining room table. We chased one another on our knees, our bellies, and on a high run, squealing and giggling mindlessly until the adults put a stop to our shenanigans. Of course, when the women went back to the kitchen and the men to their pipes and politics, we were at it again, harder than ever.

That's about all I recall of holidays at Grandma's, which is probably just as well. Our family gatherings have always been somewhat strained, if not outright hostile. The kid commotion is probably about as much fun as anyone ever had at those events.

Later on, when Grandma wasn't well enough, or perhaps after the family broke apart, we gathered at a neighbor's place; maybe stayed home if it snowed, and just ignored the day. There's no memory of special foods, other than an occasional batch of fudge or popcorn balls at Porath's or Merz's. Perhaps we weren't inclined to make so much of food, as long as there was enough of it. We were pretty busy living, and that was effort enough, without any frills.

The real celebrations were the dances, one on Christmas night, and another on New Year's Eve. These were family occasions, for those families who believed in dancing, and not everyone did. Our community contained a large proportion of folks who believed dancing was the devil's pastime. In a sense, I suppose we made a case for their belief that rowdy behavior was the essence of such gatherings. While our parents danced, we kids ran wild around the periphery of the floor or took a partner and jigged up and down to the music. It seemed to me that all our neighbors from the north-country attended those affairs but, in retrospect, I don't recall Percy Miller's family there, or having their kids included in the ragged group of rascals that wreaked mayhem and had to be told to go sit down and cool off.

Dances began at nine and ended at one a.m. The one intermission around eleven o' clock lasted for twenty minutes and allowed the men an opportunity to disperse to automobiles where they had a little nip of something to warm them. Women and kids stayed inside, and any girl who accompanied her escort out the door was sure to have her character thoroughly discussed.

Fights were common, usually fueled by overindulgence or disagreements over a woman. Any dance that didn't include fisticuffs was generally considered a disappointment. On the rare occasion when women were the participants, the whole hall emptied in a flash, although it was rare for any of the ladies to admit they had been party to such a display of impropriety.

It didn't really matter. We all knew that the fight would be conversational fodder for the week; something to alleviate the mundane flavor of our days. And that next week would provide a similar scenario, so the likelihood of boredom among the natives was slim. There was a certain rhythm to it all, and we assumed it would be ever so. None of us imagined a time when people followed their kids around to sports events or huddled at home in front of TV screens, instead of having real fun.

It Came to Pass, in Those Days...

Sally, Betty, and I lived at Grandma Spencer's that winter of 1948-49. Their little brother, John, wasn't old enough for school. When Christmas vacation arrived, Uncle Clate collected me, along with his own daughters, because the road to our place was drifted in. By then, his family was living on the Three Link, east of Brownlee, which was accessible via Highway 83 and a gravel county road. Clate had ended up with the communal pickup after we acquired a car; however, his daring to venture out on bad roads may have been simply because he was more inclined to foolhardy adventure than my practical father.

There was a phone at the Three Link but, with none at our place, my parents would have had no knowledge of the arrangements made for me. They would have just assumed that, roads permitting, we would all gather at Grandma's for Christmas Day.

On Christmas Eve we kids trailed after Clate while he milked the cow and did chores. Coming from the early winter dusk into the lamp lit kitchen, we smelled supper cooking and hurried to obey Aunt Leona's admonitions to pour water from the teakettle into a basin and wash up. The meal would have been ordinary, probably venison, or home canned beef and vegetables, along with potatoes from the cellar. We ate quickly, for my aunt had promised us a story when the dishes were done.

Presently, she took a Bible from the shelf, moved the lamp to the center of the table, and gathered us 'round. We sat spellbound as she began, "The Gospel, according to St. Luke. 'It came to pass, in those days...'"

I don't know if the reading was a tradition in their home, or if Aunt Lee simply needed to hear the words at that time in her life. We were familiar with the story from occasional exposures to

116

Sunday-School, but this seemed different because it connected us to what we were about to commemorate. The enchantment, for that's what it seemed, was likely related to hearing the words as 'story' rather than teaching.

On that long ago evening, a story transformed the dynamics in a shabby house set in a wide, lonely valley; a house that had seen little joy, but much drunkenness and despair; where in a few short years, scandal, divorce, and death would tear huge holes in the family fabric and leave scars on all of our souls.

After the reading, my cousins opened gifts. Santa had never been introduced to us, except as a character in songs and poems, and all the Spencer clan exchanged gifts on Christmas Eve so as to travel to Grandma's on Christmas Day. There were no packages under that tree for me for, of course, I was an unexpected guest, but it didn't matter. That seems strange, since I was certainly no less self-absorbed than any other nine year old. Somehow, the magic of story had transcended childish concerns.

The next morning, all six of us crowded into the cab of Clate's truck and sang *White Christmas* all the way to Grandma's, where I was reunited with my parents. We had our family celebration later. It was the year of the new bike, which I wouldn't get to ride until April, because the '49 blizzard blew in on the day I was taken back to Grandma's, and I didn't see home again for two months. That was a time of grim desperation for plains people. Many legends were born that winter, and some went untold. My dad would never say how many cattle he lost.

Soon after The Christmas Story Year, our family legends were cut off. Grownups became silent, or whispered in corners when they weren't speaking ugliness and blame. We kids were removed from one another's lives and no one addressed our grief, or gave us anything to replace the closeness we had lost. We were old enough to have understood some things if the adults had been able to tell their stories objectively. Whoever claimed that what we don't know can't hurt us was wrong.

Once upon a time, Aunt Lee read a story. The nuances of that night are easily understood from this distance. A man, already far gone in alcoholism, held it together long enough to offer a lonely only a family Christmas. A mother kept Christmas for her family in the midst of tremendous emotional turmoil. Two desperately sad adults put aside personal issues so children could be children for one more year.

My aunt and uncle never imagined they were giving me a Christmas that would stand out above all others, half a century later, but I think they would be pleased at that legacy. I know I am.

The Worst of It

The last day of Christmas vacation was sunny and warm, so mild, in fact, that Mom took a picture of me posing on the front step with my new bike, and not even wearing a coat. I hadn't had a chance to ride it yet, as the snow was too deep. Of course when the weather moderated, I'd have to take it to town because the sandy road in front of our house wasn't conducive to bicycles.

In spite of the momentary lull in wintery temperatures, Dad must have felt something in his bones, or seen it in the sky, because he hurried us a bit in getting ready to take me back to Seneca. Sure enough, before we had gone halfway, the wind had risen and the sun disappeared. Snow began drifting across the trail that had barely become drivable after the late December storms. We must have caught up with the Merz family as they returned to the school routine too, although I don't recall other cars on the road.

My parents dropped me off rather abruptly at Grandma's and headed for the hills. Sally and Betty were already in residence, so we began playing some game as the wind rose, and Grandma began looking out into the gathering dusk and falling snow. We kids started wondering if we'd get a day off from school to prolong the Christmas break, but otherwise remained unconcerned.

We did indeed get a reprieve; four days, as I recall, and when we did go to school it was all we could manage to climb over waist deep drifts in the half block trip. The wind continued, pretty much unabated, after the worst of the blizzard passed, and we surely had other days off from school. Most of what I remember from that time concerns Grandma's cousin, Ernie Shinn, popping in several times a day to see if we were all right, or if Grandma needed anything from the store, and checking her furnace. Maude and Ernie were living at Aunt Beulah's that winter. Their home was in Iowa, and I'm not sure of the reason for the extended visit. Maude's health was poor, and evidently Ernie was retired.

I don't recall how long it was before Sally and Betty got to go home for a weekend, but it was late March before I hitched a ride with Lou and Dorothy Merz. There was still no way my folks could come the three miles to get me clear home, but it was nice to be in the country. We kids played out in the snow a lot, and enjoyed walking on top of hard crusted drifts and reaching down to touch the telephone wires.

When I did get home, the story I got about my folks' adventure was a short one. They had followed Lou home as far as his place and everyone got stuck, so they all walked the last half mile to the Merz place, where they waited out the blizzard. On the third day, Dad borrowed a horse and rode home, returning a couple of days later with another horse for Mom. They rode home, and rode out the winter. I wasn't encouraged to ask any more questions, and being a self-absorbed nine-year-old, didn't pursue it. They never spoke of that time but, looking back now, I'm pretty sure they must have nearly starved to death. Surely every bit of food in the house would have been frozen, and likely the cans and jars broken. Had the milk cow dried up, or died? Had the chickens frozen to death or starved, with no one to bring food and water to them?

My mother's parents sent her clippings of articles about the blizzard of '49 from the Omaha World Herald. There are pictures of trains being dug out of drifts that towered above the locomotives and reports of people nearly freezing on passenger trains that became immobilized. No doubt Grandma and Grandpa James were frantic for news of our family, but would have had none for months. Surely Grandma Spencer was worried about my parents having started out in the beginnings of that storm, knowing the perils of travel on those marginal roads from her years of living on the ranch. She must have been concerned about how to feed three hungry and bored kids too, because I can't imagine that the store shelves contained much stock after the first few days, with no trains coming in.

Storm followed storm over the next month or two, with little respite for weary cattlemen. There were rescue planes that

120

dropped food packets and hay to remote ranches for several weeks during that hard winter, but I don't know how my folks would have gotten word out to anyone of their needs. Were there any such drops in our neighborhood? How many of our cattle perished, and how did we make it through that year with reduced income from sales?

The silence surrounding that time seems eerie, as I reflect on it now. Sandhillers love a good story, but there were few tales passed down about the '49 winter. Partly, I suppose, our parents didn't want us to know how desperate they had gotten. And just as with the Depression, those who survived had been so close to not having done so, that they were unwilling to talk about it.

It never occurred to me to ask my mother all of those questions in the last years of her life. Her memory remained strong until the end, but she might have chosen not to remember. Evidently I chose not to know, without realizing I had a choice. Maybe it was my early training from those years of information being withheld.

Here's My Heart

Mrs. Pearman placed a shoebox decorated with red and white crepe paper on her desk and told us to get ready for a Valentine's Day party. Each student was to prepare a Valentine for everyone in the room, drop it in the slot she had cut in the top of the box, and on Valentine's Day we'd exchange the contents and have cupcakes and Kool-Aid.

There were twenty odd of us in third, fourth, and fifth grades: a motley mixture of little girls in long curls or braids, scrawny urchins with scraggly hair and patched overalls, and the occasional straight A student who appeared daily in starched dresses and polished shoes.

And then there was me, painfully thin, with stringy mouse colored hair, wearing a plaid flannel shirt tucked into a wool jumper; reluctant to raise my hand when I knew the answer, which I usually did. I was the one who watched to see how it should be done, what responses garnered approval, and which girls were teased by boys who claimed to hate girls. This business of Valentines was foreign to me, but somehow I discerned it could be pretty important to one's standing in class, let alone life.

My mother went to the drugstore and came back with a packet of white paper doilies and some red construction paper. She drew a heart shaped pattern and helped me make different designs, glue them onto the doilies, and decorate them with glitter and bits of ribbon, cautioning me not to leave any student out just because they were mean or I didn't like them. Mom was big on not hurting anyone's feelings and bent on instilling the concept in her only offspring.

"Be sure to make an especially pretty one for your teacher," she reminded me. I wondered if that was because she had been a teacher and didn't get many Valentines, but having been accustomed to figuring things out on my own, didn't inquire.

The next few evenings were spent covered in glue and glitter, and in a quandary about what to write on each homemade offering. Should I just sign my name, or write, "Love, Lyn?"
After all, this was a celebration of love. Maybe I'd put my name on some and leave it off others, like the one for that stinky boy who sat across the aisle from me, and stuck his foot out to trip me whenever I stood up to recite.

I slipped my handful of Valentines into the box on the morning of the party, still worried if I'd done this right. Never having had a Valentine I couldn't guess if mine would be met with approval or ridicule.

Right after lunch, Mrs. Pearman chose the prettiest fifth grade girl and the tallest boy to open the box and distribute the contents. I noticed right off that mine were the only homemade ones. Other students had bought a packet of commercial cards with silly sayings and pictures of cuddly animals or cartoon characters. The signatures were just that, in fact some were in adult handwriting, indicating that a parent had taken on this bothersome little assignment. One or two, from girl pals, were signed with love, which made me glad I had signed mine to them the same way.

And then there was the box of little candy hearts. Who was that from? Each had a saying, some of which could conceivably be construed as affectionate. Did it come from a boy? The one I secretly liked, because he never called me names?

One might think that simple deduction would provide an answer, if all others had signatures. But there was the matter of a small heart shaped sucker, and a red foil-wrapped chocolate heart, also nameless. The sweet treats were appreciated. I valued them above store bought cards, but it was the candy hearts that held my interest, because of the messages. If there was one chance in twenty three that someone in that room regarded me as other than ordinary, I needed to know who it was.

The unsolved mystery has disappeared into the mists of wherever it is that childhood foolishness is stored. It never occurred to me to notice if everyone in the room got a box of candy hearts but, in retrospect, that's an easy case to make. No doubt there were other school parties where Valentines were exchanged, though none come to mind. But to this day I can taste those chalky bits of sugar that I savored, one by one, even unto summer vacation.

Years later, a college classmate handed me my first grown up Valentine, a heart shaped, satin covered box of chocolates, along with a proposal of marriage. The gesture was beyond all imagining. No adult male of my acquaintance indulged in such sentimentality. Perhaps I wasn't so ordinary after all.

Thirty two of those souvenir boxes came to grace a closet shelf. I learned to smile, express appreciation, and to eat chocolate, although I never had liked it much, and began to realize that sometimes sweets are bitter reminders of very ordinary betrayals.

Fun and Games

The rivers shaped our summers, and influenced the way we ordered our days at other seasons. For much of the year, the Middle Loup just slid swiftly along the north edge of Seneca, snuggling up against towering hills and minding its own. But in summer it seemed to beckon, and we willingly invaded its privacy. There were two popular swimming holes, one at the foot of the hill where the road from the north met the main bridge, and the other, known as The Rocks, a half mile or so west.

At the east end, the current was more predictable. A small meadow on the south side, between river and railroad, was lush and green, a good place to observe from if you were tired, or just too timid to attempt the diving dares going on among bigger kids. The south side was generally shallow, so we crossed the bridge after changing into our suits at Avey's house and entered the water from there. The river made no promises though, and at times we encountered deep holes, or whirlpools. "Deep" meant up to the chest, which varied with the age of the swimmer. I never learned to swim properly because my self-taught skills were dependent on the help of the current. I could eventually swim the length of a regular pool and back, but my technique didn't please the gym instructor, so I nearly flunked PE in college.

The real daredevils, mostly rowdy high school kids, hung out at The Rocks. The water wasn't much different there. There are not, and never were, any rocks in that stretch of the Middle Loup, but the area seemed sort of sinister to me. Tall trees leaned out over the south bank, and a rope had been hung from a sturdy branch, with a knot tied at the loose end. This was known as the swing, where older boys had contests, propelling themselves far out over the water before splashing into the deeper channel.

A rickety foot bridge spanned the river about halfway between the big bridges and rail crossings, and it was mostly used by students who lived north of the river. Having no real reason to tread on loose boards that lay only a couple of feet above the ripples, I was perfectly willing to delegate the adventure of stepping over missing planks to someone else.

The availability of two routes to town was convenient in the days when trains sometimes sat on the tracks for an hour at a time. After waiting five or ten minutes at the east crossing, people drove along a narrow trail beside the tracks to use the west one, knowing there was no guarantee that meanwhile the train wouldn't pull out, causing another delay for the driver. The third choice involved opening a couple of wire gates and bumping along though Avey's pasture, so it was only used by those desperate to proceed on their way.

Parents on the north side of town warned kids to never crawl under a train, even if it meant being late for school. Girls tended to comply, not so much out of obedience, as cowardice, but their brothers considered disobedience an opportunity for bragging rights. This sometimes resulted in one sibling arriving at school on time while another was tardy. Teachers seldom worried about tardiness involving those students because they had only to look out the window to know if there was a train on the tracks.

As a rule, only teachers and north side kids brought lunch to school; everyone else went home to eat. We had an hour break, and nobody on the south side lived more than five blocks away, so we gobbled our food and raced back to school to get in more play time. A ball game, cops and robbers, or swings and slide, in good weather, otherwise we played checkers, Old Maid, or board games in the classroom. Teachers either refereed or joined in. In high school we gathered around the piano and sang popular songs or old favorites. Anyone having access to sheet music donated it to the collection stored in the piano bench.

There weren't any popular girls in high school, at least not in the sense of having boys compete for their company, but there weren't any popular boys, either. Actually, there were only a handful of boys. During my two years in Seneca High, there were only five boys in high school, so it was all hands on deck for the basketball team, and if someone fouled out we finished the game with four players.

None of this is to imply there wasn't a class of misfits and odd men out, but in a sense we were all outsiders. Country kids hung out together because the town kids had always known one another, but kids who lived on the far fringes of town seemed to fall in the outcast category and joined the country bumpkins.

A handful of girls who were cute and outgoing ran in a pack. My friends and I were sure they were stuck up, and loved to discuss their character flaws, so when the groups merged for sports, or some other project, tensions ran high. Boys seemed immune to the gang mentality and mostly maintained their individuality. The other thing about boys was that they stuck together. We girls had no qualms about ratting one another out, but if boys instigated mischief and the teacher was unable to discern the culprit, the whole class was kept after school in an effort to flush out the guilty party. We girls protested the unfairness of this, but the guys remained mum.

Seneca's movie theater was a drafty old building next to the pool hall, and the one weekly showing was usually well attended. The main seats were hard and splintery; they creaked when you put the seat down and sprang up to hit the back of your legs when you stood up, but this was no concern for us. Little kids sat on backless benches at the front, and cheered at the cartoons. Our squirming and jumping up and down must have been distracting for the adults, but they were a forgiving crowd, and if it got out of hand, someone's parents came up and settled our hash.

In seventh or eighth grade we migrated to what served as a

127

balcony, more benches on a raised platform at the back. We observed the high school kids holding hands and tried to figure out when we'd be old enough to act that way, but it took a pretty scandalous performance to distract us from John Wayne on the screen.

The theater closed about the time I graduated to the balcony, and the building became a roller skating rink. That diversion wasn't my cup of tea. For some reason, the wheels on those things wanted to go in opposite directions and I was much more comfortable on ice skates.

Moving to Thedford for my last two years of high school expanded entertainment options. The theater there had a real balcony, and showed movies three nights a week. I was, by then, definitely old enough to indulge in the hand holding. There was even popcorn.

The owner catered to teenagers by playing records of the latest hits before the movie, letting us dance in a large open area at the front, and providing music for teen dances after ball games. He was single and young enough to kid around with us, while acting as an undesignated chaperone. We valued his generosity enough to behave, and I never knew anyone to be chastised or asked to leave.

Most of us had only been allowed out of the house in the first place with the warning that having privileges was contingent on our actions, and that said privileges would easily, and quickly, be rescinded if unearned. "*If you want to be treated like an adult, then act like one.*" It was a pretty good system, and worked well, until years later, when adults began acting like teenagers.

The Way We Were

This is the way we were: sunburned, tangle haired, rosy cheeked, raggedy, barefoot, out of breath, and smiling, when we weren't convulsed with laughter.

Our neighborhood was tightly knit, partly because of its location nestled in lonely ranch country, partly because of financial limitations shared by all, but largely, I think, because of generational ties: grandparents, uncles, and cousins in common, who had homesteaded north of Seneca in areas with names like Jimtown, Calf Creek, and Swan Lake.

I never fully experienced the disadvantages of being an only. To neighborhood moms and dads, I was simply part of the gang of ragamuffins running in and out, tracking mud, letting in flies, making a racket, and waiting hungrily in line for a slice of homemade bread, hot from the oven. We were disciplined, assigned chores, and loved indiscriminately.

Summer afternoons we rode horses or played in junk piles, barns, and blowouts. Sundays might find a gathering at the lake: dads supervising cane poles and bobbers, baiting hooks for the squeamish, and smoking their pipes, while moms packed up the lunch and gossiped in the shade. Before dusk, we'd be begging to stay over at one home or another, and often, the request was granted. Some nights yet, when sleep eludes me, I take myself to that old house that Billy Merz built, where giggling girls leaned on the windowsill to count stars and later fell asleep to the music of a windmill next to the cistern.

We were cautioned not to pester the hired men, but most had been putting their feet under our tables for so long they were more like uncles or big brothers to us, and pester them we did. Jerry and Ralph Van Deusen, Milt Crawford, and Earl Purdum were among the regulars. Smokey Skillings never stayed anywhere for long. His ramblings seemed to be romantically related, but we kids were pretty much kept in the dark about that. Doc and Joe Smith showed up in the community from someplace in Missouri, and stayed around a year or so, working alternately for us and the Merz families. They were young, full of fun and jokes, and shared a jalopy which got them to town on Saturday nights, but the Smiths were always back on Monday morning, bright eyed and jolly, which was a refreshing change for their employers.

The Van Deusens were a reclusive bunch. One daughter had married and moved away, but the other adults continued living with their parents on a scruffy sort of place north of Seneca, and had little visible means of support other than the boys hiring out. They were polite and soft spoken. Jerry was blind in one eye, and read his pulp westerns with the help of a magnifying glass which he allowed me to use under supervision. He also taught me to tie my shoes. Mom was left handed, and Dad had little patience with any sort of ineptness, so Jerry spent a week giving me lessons in bow tying.

Earl Purdum had been quite the cowboy in his day, but in his late years was content to run a mower in the hayfield. In his youth he had taken off for parts unknown, leaving a family to fend for themselves and, some long time later, returned as abruptly as he had left. Apparently Mrs. Earl was willing to let bygones be bygones, because they were together till his death. My mother disliked Earl, claiming he had "gotten fresh" with her, and insisted I keep my distance from him.

Milt Crawford had a family in Seneca, but his wife, Muriel, was happy to have him in the country. He was content to be sequestered on ranches for a considerable length of time but when he went to town it was anyone's guess when, or if, he'd return. If the interval of absence was unacceptable, Dad would make out a check for whatever wages he hadn't drawn and drop it off with his wife next time he was in town, so Milt would know to look for another job when he sobered up. But it was understood by all parties that if Milt needed a job some months down the road he would soon unpack in our bunkhouse again. He was good help when sober, and there's no use breaking in new employees when the one at hand already knows the routine.

Muriel taught music at our school, and liked to joke with us, but we didn't cross her. Her two boys, Mike and David, were full of the dickens and we had become used to seeing Muriel drag them home by the ear with a stick administering justice to the seat of their pants. Whatever mischief Mike and David found, their cousin Leck was usually involved in as well, but his mother was soft spoken and less public in her corrections.

John Wiley could be assumed guilty by association, and was often the real instigator. His mom, Mary Jeffords Wiley, was sometimes seen downtown on the hunt, paddle in hand. They lived with Mary's father and I don't know the circumstances around John's dad, other than that he was absent. Kids were shielded from unpleasantness as much as possible, so we just mostly enjoyed the fact that, for once, someone was in trouble besides us.

In those days, dads mostly administered discipline with a razor strap. Moms preferred a switch, often cut by the offender, or a hand to the bare bottom. Teachers usually punished by making us hold out a hand palm up, to be smacked with a ruler, or standing us at the blackboard with our noses pressed into a ring we had to draw ourselves. The high school principal kept a paddle in his desk for the worst offenders, but knowing it had holes bored in it to increase the torture was enough to deter all but the most determined scoundrel. My seventh grade teacher once brought a thick book down on the head of a recalcitrant student. It made a smack that brought the teacher from the room next door to see what was the matter, but the rest of us didn't make much of it. Gerald was always in some sort of trouble. There were mutterings among parents about bringing the incident before the school board, but as far as I know, it died a quiet death and Gerald went on being Gerald; however, we all tiptoed around Mrs. Jones thereafter.

There must have been some unwritten rule that elementary school boys were responsible for creating mayhem on a daily basis. Spitballs worked when nothing else came quickly to mind. Four of my classmates were once kept after school and made to chew a whole Sears Roebuck catalog into spit wads and throw them at the classroom clock. Neither boys nor teacher arrived home for supper that night, but the popularity of spit wads decreased exponentially.

I never heard of a parent who didn't back up a teacher's choice of consequences, and most of them added a penalty at home for any punishment meted out at school, so we kids were inclined to weigh the likely fallout of our mischief before leaping into action. Most of the time we were willing to gamble on getting off easy, and it happened just often enough to keep us creative.

At public dances, toddlers raced around the outside of the floor and later fell asleep on a pile of coats. Older kids paired off, often just two girls, to practice steps learned in the kitchen. We were apprised of appropriate behavior on reaching puberty. Young ladies saved a dance for Dad and knew that each of the neighborhood dads would appear for a turn around the floor as well. It was training in how to converse with adults. We were instructed not to turn down the homely fellow when he asked for a dance, nor anyone else, unless he was drunk, and few were.

You not only "danced with the one that brung you," (usually your dad) but went home with him too. If escorted by someone else, which was unlikely, since most families had only one vehicle, you were allowed one half hour leeway to be in the house after your parents had arrived. Any later, and it would surely be Dad who brung you for the next several occasions.

It went without saying that we'd finish high school because, for some families, ours would be the first generation to accomplish that goal. One or two girls dropped out for a year, for reasons considered routine today, but next term they were back to finish their studies, the exception being if the male component of the situation had agreed to marriage.

A few of my friends had older brothers who had quit school to enlist in World War Two, but they also returned to classes and graduated in their early twenties. After graduation we were expected to have a plan: college, a job, the military, or any combination of those—marriage too, for most of us. After all, we'd had our carefree years, intermingled with training for citizenship responsibilities. Our parents believed they had supported us long enough, and it was time to practice what we'd been taught. Whatever we hadn't learned by then soon came at us full force. Some of us did better with surprises than others, but very few of our generation became drains on society.

Reflecting on the way we were, a single word seems to summarize those times. Happy. We may not have realized it then, but perspective has to be earned, and we'd learned years ago to pay our own way.

Going Forward—or Not

Going to town was no small undertaking when I was a kid. It required a certain amount of preparation and specialized equipment. You wanted to be sure there was a shovel and jack in the vehicle. A snow scoop was for winter, a spade for summer, and woe to the person who forgot to change these tools by season. There's nothing more maddening than having to dig out of a snowdrift with a spade, and a scoop shovel is all but worthless in sand. The jack wasn't so much for flat tires as for raising the car in order to dig under it, or to place feed sacks or old boards under the tires for added traction in sand or snow.

Most people carried some sort of container to use for putting water in a radiator that boiled over, and hoped that the emergency would occur near a pond or windmill. In winter, we always included extra blankets, coats, caps, and mittens in preparation for being stuck and having to dig or, worse yet, walk for help. Actually, you probably were wearing most of the clothes you owned already; heaters weren't very efficient, so the driver often had to stop and scrape a hole in frost on his side of the windshield in order to see.

The process of countdown was useless anyhow if one hadn't prepared properly after the last outing. Most folks didn't have a garage, and wouldn't have used it if they had. Half the time the battery was so weak you needed to park on a hill and pop the clutch while rolling down, in order to start the motor. If the brakes were as weak as the battery, your start-up got pretty interesting. At our place, the hill where we parked was at right angles to the road, requiring a sharp turn at the bottom so as to keep from getting stuck in the meadow. So the drill went like this: pop the clutch, turn the key, pump the brakes quickly, and hope it all came together to make the corner without killing the engine. If all went as planned, the trip to town was on. Otherwise, we sat while Dad tinkered, in hopes of starting the motor, and since tinkering wasn't his strong suit there was always an element of surprise involved.

Most of those old cars had more power in reverse, which was a good thing. At least it made backing up that hill in our driveway easier. But often when traveling the sandy trails to town, or a neighbor's place, we'd turn around and back up a hill after a couple of failed attempts to negotiate the incline in forward gear. The trick here was to not persevere ahead so many times as to tear up the trail and make it impassable, even in reverse.

If getting stuck was inevitable, you wanted it to occur on the level, or going uphill. The worst case scenario was getting stuck on the downhill, because your only choice was to dig all the way forward through the drift or gully. By the time you were stuck, backing up was no longer an option.

By now you will have ascertained that no one in our neighborhood was fortunate enough to own any late model equipment, or even inclined to keep what they had in very good repair. Also, economizing on fuel was a priority for most. I remember the Merz men sometimes shut off the engine at the top of a long hill and coasted down. It got exciting if the engine failed to start in time to propel the car up the next incline. There were occasions when we rolled back down and sat at the bottom while the driver ground the starter.

For adults, the trips to town were as much about worry as anticipation of shopping or whatever diversion brought us out on the open road, but to us kids it seemed a grand adventure, unless we happened to be the ones dispatched to get help when all options had been exhausted.

My mother was always a nervous wreck when a journey occurred in bad weather, and rightfully so, because Dad would never have come looking for us if we hadn't arrived in a timely manner. Some of the husbands were a bit more considerate, or perhaps their wives had them better trained. They might follow the women and kids in a second vehicle, at least until it was pretty certain that the worst places had been negotiated.

One stormy Friday, Lou Merz came to Seneca to escort his family home to the ranch for the weekend. They had to use the snow road, which wound through several pastures before joining the main track at Calf Creek valley. Lou went ahead in the jeep to break trail that was quickly drifting in; opening gates, driving through, and waiting while the second vehicle passed through, whereupon one of the kids shut the gate before going on.

Dottie Merz, who was about twelve at the time, had been riding with her dad. She opened the gate onto Calf Creek flat and waited for her mother to pass. Both parents assumed she had gotten in the other vehicle, and both drove off, leaving her alone in the dusk and swirling snow. She only had to walk a half mile to the Prindle place, but it was a cold and scary half mile, and by the time the family got home and discovered the mistake the phone was ringing. One angry daughter had plenty to say about her adventure, and both parents were backing up.

Afoot, and Okay with That

It wasn't uncommon, in the 1940's, for families not to own a car. Most of Seneca's population traveled by train if they went out of town but there was little reason to leave town. Mullen had a dental office and a country doctor, but you could get on a train to go there and back in a day. Doc Walker (both the MD and his dentist son were Doc Walkers) made house calls, but most people dosed themselves with home remedies and got well on their own, or had someone haul their broken bones to his office to be set. Pretty much everything one needed was available in Seneca, including a coffin, if you were inconsiderate enough to die.

It seemed that the majority of vehicles were owned by young bucks just back from the war. Folks mostly got around town on foot, and if the family had wheels, and the father worked out of town, his wife used shanks mares anyhow. A majority of the dads who lived in town worked for the railroad and didn't really need a car to get to their jobs.

Our jointly owned pickup was just for making trips to town for supplies, or going back and forth between Clate's place and ours. You couldn't have negotiated that road in a regular automobile then, and still can't, so a lot of travel in our vicinity was powered by equines. For a long time, we didn't go far enough, often enough, to make other arrangements necessary. Any ranch work, such as fencing, feeding, or checking water, was done with horses.

It seems strange to think that my grandmother spent a couple of decades widowed and self-supporting, with no form of motorized transportation. As far as I know, she never learned to drive, however I think not many women of her generation did drive. The little old ladies we visited on lonely winter evenings didn't have cars either. Some had husbands or bachelor sons who drove them; others just walked everywhere, like Grandma.

Many of the mothers of my friends may not have driven, but it hadn't occurred to me to question that circumstance. If my classmates' families had cars, it was always a father at the wheel. Ranch women drove out of necessity, but maybe their town sisters did not. I don't recall Mildred Porath or Donaldine Avey driving the family car uptown for groceries, but I don't remember them walking either. My sense is that they stayed home in the kitchen or garden, and the men or kids did errands. A lot of kids came to school with a grocery list in their pockets and picked up the order on the way home. Everyone had a charge account at the general store, so they didn't need to carry money.

These were not helpless or dependent women. Grandma supported herself for years by taking in boarders, as did many other housewives of the day. Some did outside washing or sewing, or gave music lessons, and all of them raised gardens, canned, and created the family's wardrobes. They could organize a church fundraiser and provide music or write skits for school programs. Whether they were going "over town" for business or social purposes, they walked. They never went to the kid's ball games, out to eat, or to movies. Were their lives narrow? Did they feel trapped, or deprived? If so, I never got a hint of it.

Perhaps they didn't have time to consider any other lifestyle. My mom had little free time, but having grown up in another culture she felt the differences keenly. Our home was full of books, magazines, and newspapers, so she kept up with the changes in urban life, but had little opportunity to participate in it. In her adopted world, the men belonged to Masons and the women to Eastern Star or garden clubs. Social life for town women was church and 4-H meetings, but I could hear plenty of gossip while sitting under a quilt frame in Grandma's dining room when her Ladies Aid Society met there,

The only times I remember Grandma going out of town was one or two Christmases when Dad or Uncle Clate brought her

138

to the ranch for the day, or if one of her other sons came to get her for a visit in Scottsbluff or Wyoming.

Grandma had suffered from motion sickness on the way to several new homes, whether by wagon or on trains, and sympathized with my similar tendency, hoping I'd outgrow it. I did, but she never hinted that she had, so perhaps it was a blessing for her to travel under her own steam. That doesn't answer for the other women. Maybe it was simply the notion that one ought to be content in whatever circumstance they had chosen. Whatever the case, I can't muster up pity or sorrow for them, probably because they didn't indulge in it for themselves. There's a lesson for us in that.

Take it Out of Overdrive

Even after half a century, my city born mother never learned to drive Sandhill roads with any degree of confidence. She'd been a resident for several decades before we had anything but two track trails to travel, so every trip to town was a nerve wracking deal for her and anyone who rode along.

There were numerous sandy hills to be negotiated between the ranch and town. Where the road followed the edge of a meadow, you could count on bottomless ruts when it rained, and on curves sheltered by trees the snow drifted deep, no matter which way the wind blew.

Most people would decipher the code; learn where to detour around soft spots, which hill required gearing down and "taking a run at it" so as not to be stuck halfway to the top, and when to downshift on steep slopes to keep from sliding into a ditch. But Mom was always so nervous she couldn't remember what had gotten her into a fix the last time, so it was generally "same song, second verse" unless blind luck happened to favor her on any given day. Now, mind you, my mother was an intelligent and well educated woman. She had her share of common sense too, but in the matter of trail navigation, there was a curtain of denial which made her believe that using the same method every time would result in different outcomes.

Dad could never contain his disgust when he had to go haul her out of another mess, and this factor simply added to her apprehension and made her more likely to find trouble where it well might have been avoided. He seldom got stuck, partly due to experience and a photographic memory for where trouble spots in the road always occurred. But the main difference was that he downshifted and slowed up when he anticipated difficulty, whereas Mom put the pedal to the metal, and trusted simple speed to get her through. What this philosophy actually did was put her closer to the middle of disaster, rather than on the edge of it.

When Dad started down the steep hill on the north edge of Seneca that ends at the railroad tracks, he "put 'er in low" and crept along. It was overkill, but he never ended up in the ditch from riding the brakes if it was icy or landed in the lake like a couple of well-oiled travelers once did.

My father took a lot of ribbing about his turtle speed, but he usually got where he was going on time, because he left early in order to make up for it. Dad had another idiosyncrasy too; he never bought on credit. We did without a lot of the frills our neighbors enjoyed, but we never had to worry about a note being called. Mom, on the other hand, could pinch a penny about so long, and then needed to find a higher gear.

I guess you could say their driving habits resembled the way they handled finances. Now and then, Mom just had to put it in overdrive, and Dad was always sitting alongside telling her to slow down.

Don't Ask, Don't Tell

I didn't know what the fight was about, and something in the manner in which I was informed of it warned me not to ask. Maybe it was the awareness that my mother's propensity to one sided reporting about matters that riled her meant that whatever explanation was given would be less than accurate. More likely, I simply didn't want the graphic details leading up to my dad's black eye and split lip; having to hear that he got the worst of it, or that Clate, in a drunken state, had committed some unforgivable act and gotten thrown off the place.

Dad and his next older brother had already dissolved the ranch partnership with their mother, so it was unlikely to have involved business. All I was told was that Clate had come to our place, there had been a fight, and we would no longer associate with that family.

I was boarding at Porath's when it happened, probably about the time the old bunkhouse burned, because from then on I always felt like an outsider in our family. Every important event seemed to happen while I was away at school: trials of the '49 blizzard, family divisions, the burning bunkhouse, and efforts to save it. My Uncle Floyd, Aunt Iva's husband, died of cancer in Omaha, and I didn't even know he'd been sick. Grandpa James had a heart attack, Mom lost the sight in one eye; these were reported to me briefly, with no details supplied. Life went on around me while I watched from the sidelines.

Uncle Floyd was buried with none of us attending. Grandpa got well, retired, and lived a couple more decades, and Mom got stronger glasses. They cleaned up debris from the bunkhouse fire and planted a garden on the spot. Hired hands slept in the hayloft the next summer while the new bunkhouse was being built, and Dad bought a new car to put in the garage side of it. I eased into more responsibility in family matters; took over ironing for the family to avoid Mom's complaints about heating sad irons on the kitchen range, and saddled up to ride the south pastures checking windmills or fence.

It was easy to pretend not much about our lives was changing, except for the hole left by the lack of cousin connections. Sally and Betty were no longer my playmates. I missed knowing what they looked like growing up, what they liked to do, and where they went to school. Leona divorced Clate along in there someplace, and they moved away, but the divorce was little mentioned, and only in whispers when I was present. It was long years later, and not from parents, that I learned details of the bitter court battle. The customary holiday dinners at Grandma Spencer's, ended then. Whether my parents distanced themselves, or we were disinvited, I can't say.

There were other hints of family unrest. I was allowed glimpses of those, perhaps because the folks wanted to diminish the effect of any neighborhood gossip. Not to worry. The neighbors minded their own, or at least didn't discuss our business in the presence of kids.

Dad mentioned having paid off the mortgage on the ranch. Mom said that Dad's brother Fred and Beulah's son Courtney were trying to take the ranch away from us, but I wasn't told if the case ever went to court, or why the relatives wanted it. I'd never known either of them to set foot on the place in my lifetime.

But with that controversy, another door closed. We no longer celebrated the Fourth at Beulah's or went to Scottsbluff to visit Fred's. Somewhere in that time frame, Beulah's son Spencer and his wife divorced, and cousins from that marriage disappeared from my life, too. I wasn't party to the reasons for that split; once more I met the impenetrable wall of silence, felt the loss of connections, and knew that asking would only get me that old song and dance about being too young to bother about such things.

That excuse worked well for kids, but I'm an adult now and, for whatever reason, I still haven't asked. Pretty much anyone who would have answers to the questions has long since died. The cousins of my generation don't have a clue about most of these mysteries either. Whether we were all well trained in silence and secret keeping, I can't say, but sometimes I wonder. If knowledge is power, how many of my own mistakes might have been avoided if I hadn't been scared to ask more questions?

Shall We Dance, Or Would You Rather Fight?

Shortly after Mom came to teach in Seneca, Dad invited her to a Saturday night dance. She turned him down because her college professors had firmly maintained that school teachers weren't to indulge in pastimes such as card playing and dancing. He laughed at that, informed her she wasn't in the city anymore, and said that out here everyone danced if they felt like it. So it was that their first date was for a public dance in the Seneca auditorium, located just behind Dad's mother's house, where Mom and another teacher had room and board.

There were dances in Seneca or a neighboring town most Saturday nights, and always on holidays. Some of my earliest memories involve those dances, the music swirling my parents out on the floor into a blur of color and grace while I cried pitifully at being relegated to the sidelines. I'm not sure whether my tears were a result of separation or a need to be among the throng of dancers, but Dad usually scooped me up on their next pass, holding me in one arm as they danced while I relaxed and let the music move through me. I remember lying in bed at my grandmother's house with music and laughter floating through the open window, along with echoes of my mother's parting comment. *"No. This time your dad and I are going alone."* But those disappointing episodes were rare because shortly past toddler stage we kids began to venture out on the floor in groups. We were a serious hazard to other dancers, but no one scolded us, and if we got run over it was likely our own fault because the adults were proficient at maneuvering around us.

Later on, our parents began teaching us. Little girls might learn by standing on Daddy's boots. Boys were instructed to hold out a hand and ask a lady politely, escort her back to her seat after the music ended, and thank her for the dance. I don't recall being informed that it was time to stop running around the floor with the little kids, but somehow the message was transported that more

145

ladylike comportment was in order.

Single men lounged in a loosely organized stag line just inside the door, looking over the prospects while women and girls sat primly in chairs placed along the walls waiting to be chosen. I sat a lot, except when Dad or one of my friends' fathers came to my rescue.

After an hour of this, we unpopular girls usually gave up and danced with one another. It beat sitting all night, but we still went home with our self-esteem dragging around our ankles. Older women said it was rude to turn down a request to dance unless the man was drunk, but it was hard to tell how drunk someone was until you were halfway round the floor. Since the dilemma was seldom presented to me, it was of little concern.

Intermission came around midnight and lasted long enough for the menfolk to disperse to their automobiles for a nip of joy juice. Women and girls remained indoors, except for the occasional flashy dresser who accompanied her date out the door. These would be labeled "fast" by those of us who kept track, but it didn't seem to modify their tendency to depart on future occasions.

The main diversion for intermission, other than drinking, was fisticuffs. Any dance that didn't include a fight was considered a disappointment. On rare occasions women were involved—generally the ones who fell into the "fast" category.

Occasionally, a disagreement got ahead of itself when the combatants couldn't postpone their conflict until intermission. Someone would appear in the doorway and yell, "FIGHT!" and the stag line melted magically while the band tried mightily to ignore the distraction. Couples continued dancing, with the female partner attempting to retain her man's attention in spite of the fact that his head kept swiveling toward the door. You knew he was dying to find out who was involved in the altercation and whether, if it was one of his buddies, his assistance might be required. But there was this woman hanging on for dear life; a date who would claim desertion if abandoned, or a wife unhappily reminding him of the black eye he sustained after the last episode into which he had inserted himself. Where does a fellow's loyalty lie, anyway?

One by one, men escorted a partner to the sideline and abandoned ship. Eventually the band put down their instruments and joined the exodus. The women, having lost another round, resigned themselves to it gracefully, roaming about to chat, demonize younger females who had gone out to view the fracas, or vow by all that was holy to let their individual fools rot in jail, should the sheriff charge them with being drunk and disorderly.

Generally, the interruption was brief. Either the law intervened, or one of the pugilists cried uncle after his opponent's buddies ganged up on him. Returning musicians swung into something lively, like *Redwing*, and apologetic spouses sheepishly reclaimed their partners. Those of us wallflowers who had sat unnoticed through the whole deal waited for the popular gals to come over and share juicy details of who won, and whether the disagreement involved an ongoing feud or just some ill-advised comment that served as an excuse for excitement in an otherwise ordinary gathering. Those customs are long gone, and the dynamics of our community changed so gradually that we barely noticed, but I'm inclined to believe the old days were a lot more fun.

Dancing With the Devil

On this chilly March Sunday we leave on our wraps for a while, huddled around the stove that sits in the parlor of the parsonage. It's a modern heater for the times, shiny brown metal, with the name of the manufacturer on the front in raised silver toned letters. Kerosene warmth radiates onto the tan and brown speckled linoleum, lying unevenly on the old wood flooring, and I step out of my penny loafers to feel it on the sole of my white anklets.

As soon as the chill has gone, I remove my jacket. Today I have worn the electric blue taffeta dress with dainty white lace around its Peter Pan collar, and I want to show it off to my Sunday-School classmates.

The preacher's wife teaches our class. He is Brother Jones, so naturally she is Sister Jones. We are the intermediates, grades four through six. Primary and preschoolers are in the kitchen. Juniors, seventh through high school, meet next door in the white frame church, in the back two rows, while the adult class is up front.

Sister Jones hands out our Sunday-School papers and we take turns reading the lesson aloud. Brightly colored images of people in turbans, sandals, and robes are mingled with the text, and there's a memory verse printed at the top. All of us have memorized the one from last week, and we chant it while I smooth wrinkles from the skirt of my blue dress. I'm bored with this and wish I was old enough to return in the evening for the Young People's meeting.

Dismissed, we trek across the yard to the church, stepping gingerly around puddles and patches of dirty snow. I take my seat at the front as the piano begins the opening strains of Amazing Grace. "Next year," I think, "I'll be sitting in the back row with the young people, where Carol is right now; holding hands with Reuben under a hymn book."

***

It will be some time before my mind opens to philosophies other than the ones being presented in the social structure which formed life with the Porath family, but for the time being, it made a good framework in which to grow and form a picture of the world. Never having to question; having everything presented as being black and white, simplified our lives. Today I wonder if folks in that church worried about world hunger, injustice, racial strife, or domestic violence. Did anyone ever consider whether God might be black or possibly female? They all accepted some brand of Christianity as the only route to heaven, disagreeing only on matters like whether to permit makeup or dancing, and whether it was ok to pray to the Virgin Mary. Non-believers, or at least non-church goers, were lumped with the heathen in Africa.

It wasn't long though, before I began to question how their God could damn my dad, who didn't like to go to church and did like to dance, but was the kindest man I knew, or for that matter, those half-clad children in National Geographic who had obviously never heard of Jesus.

What was the hang up about that dance thing, anyhow? My parents danced, and music lived in my feet. How could such joy be a work of the devil? Dance I would, I decided, and be damned, if it came to that.

A Fool's Game

Mrs. Crain taught sixth, seventh, and eighth grades in an upstairs room adjacent to the three rooms which comprised Seneca High School. Hers was a lively venue, not only because middle school kids are mostly unmanageable, but also because the door to the fire escape was in our room. It opened onto a metal tube attached to the outside of the building, and you slid down the tube whenever there was a fire drill. We liked knowing that we got first chance at the sliding; the only way to get one up on the stuck up high school bunch, who had to file in quietly and wait their turn. Sometimes we attempted to climb up the tube and enter our room by that door, but it was frowned on and, if caught, the punishment could be severe, so we quit bothering with that. It wasn't much of a challenge anyway.

We didn't often test Mrs. Crain's determination that her students would eventually become civilized humans, probably, in part, because she made learning fun, but now I realize what a trial we must have been. A single teacher for three grade levels couldn't have been a picnic, but that was the norm for small town schools and she took it in stride.

Her decision to teach us the waltz during PE class was a welcome change from the usual jumping jacks and toe touches, at least for the girls. We didn't mind that the needle on her record player was worn, and sometimes stuck, requiring us to begin the exercise all over again.

"Raymond, put your arm around Melba's waist. She won't bite!" Raymond complied, but kept a safe distance just in case, while Mrs. C. pretended not to notice.

"Darrell, you're out of step again. Start over and count with me. One two three, one two three...
"Elizabeth, you'll have to be a boy this time, there aren't enough to go around and you're taller than Shirley. No, you lead

with your left foot, like this…"

My classmates may not have viewed this exercise as a rite of passage, but I was stepping into a magical dream that led straight to the center of the floor. At long last I'd have dancing partners for Saturday nights. But a couple of important details had escaped me. Not every family in our small community danced; in fact, many of my fellow students were members of a denomination that frowned on such worldly pastimes. In addition, the people in my parents' close circle of friends were, well, different.

Our country neighbors helped one another with work, played cards in winter, fished in summer, and danced most Saturday nights, so we kids spent a considerable amount of time together. We were kind of a motley crew, but none of us had had occasion to give it much consideration.

Percy and Vivian Miller were seldom at dances. Wendell Merz had been assigned the role of prodigal son by his siblings, as a result of having gone off to travel the world as a young man before returning to work the ranch with his brother, and marry. Their son, Jerry, was enough older to seem nearly invisible to me. Their family danced, and I suppose Jerry attended, as well, but he wouldn't have hung out with the kid sister gang.

Lou and Dorothy Merz had the care of Billy and his wife, Anna. Lou kept busy enough to seem on the fringes of daily life, and Lord knows, Dorothy had her hands full, so we kids had the run of the place. I, the oddball kid, interacted as a unit with their offspring. Although Larry was close in age to his cousin Jerry, he had limited mental capabilities. Dottie, four years my senior, was also a bit behind the curve, and close enough to my interests that we got along well. Shirley, the youngest, was lively, intuitive, and so normal that we decided she fit the category of little brat. I suppose the rest of us felt our inadequacies so deeply that a scapegoat seemed necessary. My mother had drilled into me that I was never to treat Larry and Dottie differently, and I didn't. In fact, they were the children I played with most often and understood best.

These were the people who accompanied us to dances. Not that cute boy who sat ahead of me in school. Not the basketball star or even my best friend from town, whose handsome cousin always came to spent the summer. Even though I now knew the steps, suddenly dances weren't as much fun. We were given the new rules about girls having to wait to be asked and never leaving the dance hall. Now we really were the odd ball crew, but I never considered staying away. Music was the magic carpet that floated all my fantasies.

Our fathers claimed dances with each of us, just as they danced dutifully with each of the neighbor wives. I preferred dancing with my friends' dads, because my own tended to instruct me in the same manner he used when teaching me to drive.

Occasionally some drifter with beer breath took us for a twirl but mostly we pasted on smiles, tapped our feet in time with the music to show interest, and cast furtive glances at the stag line. Our hearts beat faster when an interesting looking lad moved in our direction, and sank like stones when he held out a hand to the pretty girl sitting nearby, who would certainly disappear at intermission.

Most of the dancing we did was with each other. Dottie was pretty good, but never mastered the art of leading, so I always had to be the boy. Shirley and the younger bunch hung out together and ignored us. Larry always asked me to dance three or four times, and true to my training, I accepted, knowing that association likely eliminated any chance of getting asked by the fellows I'd been eyeing. Actually, he wasn't a bad dancer and it beat sitting. Heaven knew I was no prize myself: skinny, awkward, and shy, with unruly dishwater blond hair.

During our high school years, the moms stayed in town with us during the week. By then, Larry had dropped out of school to help Lou on the ranch. Everyone else departed for the ranches on Friday and migrated back to civilization Sunday evening. Sometimes, when the parents didn't plan to attend a Saturday night dance, the Merz girls and I begged to remain at their town house for the weekend. Since we hadn't shown enough creativity in the mischief department to keep the request from being granted, those Friday nights were spent indulging in popcorn while listening to the radio and practicing our dance steps. On Saturday we ironed our best dresses, laid out jewelry, and fixed our hair while harmonizing on songs we'd hear later that evening.

Anticipation was building by the hour. Surely this would be the night a handsome stranger would hold out his hand and claim every dance for the rest of the evening. I don't think it was even about romance, at least for me. Just the notion of never having to sit out a dance was beyond my wildest dreams.

Nine o'clock found us at the door of the dance hall, getting our hands stamped; unnecessary, since we remembered that only bad girls go out at intermission, and no one was going to ask us to anyhow. But the ticket taker wouldn't know that, and it made us feel grown up.

Not having the dads on deck meant that we'd sit more than usual, but hope springs eternal in teenage breasts, and when the music began anything seemed possible. Our illusions faded slowly as the night wore down, and disappeared entirely when the lights were dimmed and the band swung into *Let Me Call You Sweetheart*, followed by *Good Night Ladies*.

One more time, we were no one's sweetheart, but we could still be ladies, so we smiled brightly and slipped out the side door, making plans for the Thanksgiving Dance, a couple of weeks away. Walking the few blocks home, we sang our favorite songs again. Number one on the charts for many of those months was a tune called, *A Fool Such As I*. We knew all the words. I still do.

One Old New Year's Eve

I really hadn't much experience at being a brat; in fact, I'd always made a concerted effort to disprove the theory that only children tend to be self-centered and spoiled. But despite the lack of practice, on New Year's Eve of 1954 I was surprisingly good at making an exception to that vow.

We had been in town all day so Dad could be at the bedside of his mother, whose 93 year old body was shutting down. I consigned this concern to the world of adults, which was not unusual, since our family was disinclined to include youngsters in serious discussions. I don't know if that was out of consideration for sparing us worry, or simply the notion that kids and adults should each mind their own business.

Full of energy and carefree as only teenagers can be, my friends and I had cast off our coats and spent the unseasonably balmy day climbing the bluffs above the river, jumping off into blowouts and discussing what to wear to the dance that night.

My assumption that I'd be attending the dance was based on tradition, but also had to do with the attention paid me by a particular male companion at a dance a couple of weeks previously. Mind you, I don't recall the person's name, age, or anything else about him, including whether there had been mention of seeing me again, but high school sophomores don't need much evidence to get their imaginations going.

At dusk, my companions and I dispersed. Returning to the two rooms in the upstairs of a big old house where Mom and I stayed during the school week, I was informed that I would not be going anywhere that evening. It wasn't a matter of my walking a few blocks alone or even returning alone in the wee hours. Seneca wasn't a place where we worried about such things and, in any event, I probably could have accompanied the Merz family. But

Dad was convinced his mother wouldn't survive the night, and for me to be out having fun at such a time was improper, not to mention disrespectful.

This was a side of my father that I hadn't encountered, and I didn't take it lying down, for all the good it did me. He was right, of course, but I argued for all I was worth, pouted, and finally went to bed in tears, making sure my sobs would be audible across the hall. About midnight, my grandmother's caretaker called up the stairs to tell Dad that his mother had died, and a few days later we attended the funeral. Still smarting from my disappointment, I wasn't attuned to the emotions and dynamics of a family who, at best, were barely tolerant of one another. The service passed in a blur, although I was conscious of an undercurrent of guilt, or at least the realization that such a feeling would have been appropriate on my part.

Obviously, any earlier attempts to pass myself off as considerate and helpful had been little more than a cover-up for the person I really was. I'm pretty sure I never apologized to my parents for being such a self-centered little twit. It certainly takes a long time for some of us to grow up. By the time I did, the people to whom I owe that apology had joined my grandmother.

IceCapades

I unearthed the scuffed black hockey skates from a dark corner of the garage sometime during the winter of my freshman year in high school. The blades were rusty and the leather so limp that when I put them on and stood up, my ankles turned and nearly upended me.

"Where did these come from?" I asked Mom. "Did you used to ice skate?"

"No, those were my brother's," she replied. "I don't know why I ended up with them."

"Can I have them?"

"Sure, but where will you use them?"

"On Hardy's lake in town, but I'll practice on the creek out front first."

Over the next several years, I managed to disprove the saying that practice makes perfect, but nobody ever had as much fun practicing as I did with those skates. The ice on the creek in our meadow was rough and full of holes, punctuated by weeds that stuck out every few feet, and inclined to break through in shallow spots, but I eventually got so I could glide along fairly well without falling or having my ankles betray me.

A few of my classmates had gotten skates that year—real figure skates that had stiff uppers for supporting ankles. Others had hand-me-downs that were too big, and required them to wear several pairs of socks so the skates would halfway fit. Those who didn't have skates simply slid around on their shoes.

There was nothing formal about our gatherings on the lake

down by the railroad tracks, and I don't recall any advance planning. Our rooms in town looked out on the lake so I could see when someone was there, and if it was dark, the light from a bonfire of old tires the boys had scrounged up alerted me to a party in progress. On any given night, when ice wasn't covered with snow, a dozen kids of various ages congregated to play crack the whip or hang around the fire and warn latecomers of places where the ice was thin due to springs at the west end. Occasionally, someone brought marshmallows to roast and no one seemed to notice an aftertaste of burnt rubber. If the moon was full we didn't need a fire for light, but it was generally so cold we lit one anyhow and braved the smoke to warm at least one side of ourselves.

Helen Avey had a pair of new white figure skates and, as a natural athlete, soon was the star of our ice show, twirling around in the firelight, showing us how to skate backwards, and grabbing a partner to skate double. I envied her skates but knew I'd be making do with Vance's legacy, and cherished no illusions that new skates would ever make me as good as Helen.

Years later, my husband got me white figure skates for Christmas. By then I was mom to four kids, and supposedly a responsible adult but, when I laced them up and stood on the ice, I felt like I was fourteen again. For the next few years our family gathered often on Swan Lake for skating parties with the Merz clan or at the Brownlee Bayou with the kids' classmates. Sometimes we built a fire to roast hot dogs and marshmallows, or a parent supplied hot chocolate. Yes, parents attended too; even the fathers got skates, and at least pretended to participate.

One year, we had planned a New Year's Eve get together with Merzes, on a pond in our meadow, but the day before our outing it snowed six inches, leaving no open ice. Our family grabbed shovels and shop brooms and cleared enough ice so the celebration could proceed on schedule under a perfect full moon.

I disremember, but imagine the dads treated themselves to a

nip of firewater while warming their backsides by the fire and the rest of us drank hot chocolate. That was the best of New Year's Eves, and even made up for missing the dance the year Grandma Spencer died.

Out on the Town

It seemed like our parents were too busy to bother with us, which suited everyone fine. Oh, there were rules aplenty—no back talk, get your chores done, change your clothes after school, be home before supper, and wash behind your ears. Don't get in trouble at school or you'll be in worse trouble at home. But everyone's folks had the same rules, so it wasn't like I could go over to a friend's house and get by with anything. We knew our friends' parents wouldn't hesitate to rat us out so, as long as we stayed out from underfoot, everyone was comfortable and the system for keeping us in line was pretty successful.

Our time was pretty much our own once school was out and chores were done. Homework didn't exist, unless you'd been out sick. Teachers kept us in at recess, or after school, until our work was handed in, and staying after qualified as getting in trouble at school. If a sibling didn't tattle about mid-day detention you might get by okay, but arriving home a half hour late required some uncomfortable explanations.

Bad weather was about the only thing that kept us indoors, and it had to be pretty bad before we gave up roaming the streets in search of someone else at loose ends and up for a bike ride, ball game, or just hanging out at the swings on the school grounds. Technically, no one was supposed to be on the school grounds when teachers weren't present, so if some nosy mom happened to look out the window and feel compelled to make a report, there could be consequences.

By the time I reached high school, Dorothy Merz had a house in town and my own mom was in residence down the street. The latter to keep an eye on me, I was sure, and it was probably true, but the interesting thing was how the women occasionally went home on weekends and let us stay at the Merz house in order to attend a ball game or dance. This made no sense, other than allowing the parents some private time, and that may have been the real motive. In any case, we took it and ran. Dottie Merz was two grades ahead, so perhaps the parents considered her capable of keeping Shirley and me in line, which everyone, including ourselves, realized was no trick. What were we going to do? All of us were plain, shy, and unpopular, so a gathering of our peers would hardly happen at that house. Such a notion never occurred to us, and anyway Mrs. Parrish lived right next door and she and Dorothy had coffee together often. The Merz family had telephones at the ranch, and in town, but I don't recall anyone ever calling to check on us.

Why did we want to stay in town when all of us loved being home on the ranch? I think now, it was about music. Like all teens, we were consumed by it. Dorothy had a piano (pronounced pie-ann-o in that house) and Bob Edelman lived a couple of doors down. He could play anything by ear, but had no piano at home, so often dropped by for a songfest or a ball game in the vacant lot across the street. Bob was handsome, and every girl in school had a crush on him, but he attended the church that didn't believe in dancing, and anyhow, he only dated the pretty girls. He was the only boy I remember that would give Larry Merz the time of day. He always included Larry in our ball games and engaged him in conversation, at least briefly. Why he hung out with our bunch of misfits is beyond me, but it occurs to me now that I never saw him in the company of the rowdy gang of mischief makers during off-school hours. We might have been his only choice for leisure companions. His parents were elderly and his siblings were all grown and gone. It seems likely that his mother kept a pretty tight rein, and with the Merz house and vacant lot where we played ball only a few steps from his home, mamma could pretty well track his activities. He was a pretty quiet kid, though, and perhaps just didn't care for the rough and tumble crowd. He never joined us at the skating parties or swimming holes, either.

Staying in town of a weekend didn't require attending

Sunday-School but we always did because it was another chance to sing. Seneca had few sidewalks so we usually walked in the middle of the street. Once, on the way home from church, we heard a loud motor behind us and quickly moved to one side so the vehicle could pass. Turning, we saw a small plane taxiing toward Main Street. No surprise. Seneca's saloon was the only one for miles that was open on Sunday, and Charlie Swanson was known for his powerful thirst.

I Know It's True; I Heard It Twice

I don't know when the phone line from Seneca to our community was put in or who did the work. Probably it was a group effort by the folks who believed they would benefit from better communication, but obviously my dad wasn't among that company. It was fine with him to be out of the loop, and he knew the word from down the road would eventually reach our doorstep. Until then he was content to mind his business.

From my youthful perspective, it seemed that homegrown phone line was almost more trouble than it was worth; at least my playmates' fathers spent a lot of time on maintenance. Since the wires were strung on fence posts or tall poles salvaged from a corral, a sag, or break, was apt to occur anytime there was high wind or heavy snow, and lightning was a culprit too. When the women reported that the phone was out, (naturally, women were the first to discover such catastrophes) husbands were dispatched immediately to find the problem and fix it.

Connections were often crackly and unclear, but information got passed along in a timely manner because it was a party line, and ranch wives kept current with gossip by listening in. I've no clue why this was called "rubbering." Most women participated but no one admitted doing it, even though you could hear receivers being picked up, and every extra person who came on the line diminished the quality of the connection.

Each home had a distinctive ring: a long and two shorts, one long, or some variation of such, so you always knew who was being called, and whether or not that conversation might be of enough interest to stop what you were doing and listen. Everyone knew who the worst busy-bodies were which led to occasional animosity.

"Clara? Is that you again? Please hang up. This is long

distance and it's hard enough to hear."

Clara complied with the request, but curiosity usually got the best of her in a few moments, whereupon she picked up again, as quietly as possible, and earned another rebuke.

Rubbering was considered a womanly vice, and men joked about it, but we all knew certain men who were addicted. It was pretty much a given that when a husband passed on a juicy bit of neighborhood news he had been eavesdropping, or was married to Clara.

Surely the neighbors invited Dad to be part of the phone coop when it began but he, or perhaps his father, opted out. When our children were small, Bob and I decided a phone was a priority and paid for the labor and materials to connect with the line out of Brownlee, but Dad refused to participate. Mom could have her phone, and did, but only if the listing didn't include Dad's name. Still, he must have known the modern world would catch up with him because they had already built the new house which had a shelf specifically for a phone.

The line we connected with had as many subscribers as the one from Seneca, but being busy with kids and outdoor work, I seldom bothered to listen in. In fact, there were times when I buried the darn thing under a pillow so as not to have it wake a napping toddler.

There were a couple of ladies on that line who rivaled Clara in time spent gathering news. Upon hearing Mattie and Harry Higgins' or George and Rachel Higgins' rings, we knew to go ahead and weed the garden, or do the milking, because it was going to be a while before the line was free.

Rachel was a good hearted, easy going soul. Since she and George had no children I suppose she had more time to spend on the phone. The sisters-in-law got along famously, and checked in regularly with one another.

George was a wiry little Irishman who enjoyed a visit as much as his wife, but he preferred to do it in person, over a wee nip. In those days, most ranchers carried a pint of something under the pickup seat for medicinal purposes, or just to be social. In case of meeting a neighbor along the road it was customary for both vehicles to stop; windows would be rolled down, pipes lit, or a sack of Bull Durham opened, and the bottle offered.

George's stock was most likely a fifth, rather than a pint; therefore it tended to roll around more when he hit a bump. Now, every woman knew about their mates' secret stash, but pretended not to. Rachel was the exception. She considered it her duty to monitor George's intake, and he got pretty good at foiling her efforts. When they went to town, Rachel went to the grocery store and George headed for the bar, the understanding being that he could have two drinks while she shopped. Rachel hurried through her list and soon presented herself at the bar to collect George, who had also hurried with his priority. He would be just finishing his drink when she arrived, announcing it was time to head home. It should be noted that her presence in such an establishment was unusual since women, excepting those of a certain reputation, didn't appear in bars. However, Rachel was well aware that if she didn't insist, her errant spouse wouldn't emerge until closing time. Likely she was also aware that he could drink faster than she could shop.

"Come on George, it's time to go."

"Aw Rach, wait just a minute. This is my first, and you know I always have two." (Wink at the bartender, as the glass was refilled.)

Rachel was stumped. She had no proof, after all, and arguing was pointless. It would become apparent just how many

George had downed when he arose from the stool, swaying slightly but, for now, none of his drinking buddies were talking and their grins were well hidden.

Rachel had learned to check under the seat as well, and at one point was sure she'd disposed of all his secret supply. On the way home from somewhere George hit a pothole, and out rolled a bottle. No one knows what was said in the conversation that ensued, but word about the incident got around the neighborhood. Chances are Rachel's daily conversations with Mattie had something to do with that.

Dad liked Rachel a lot. She had spunk and was independent, qualities he admired in women. But he also liked to tell stories on her. According to him, one day George had gone to town alone and tied one on. He got home very late, bringing someone with him. It's hard to say which of the bad boys was in the worst condition but, having been too busy drinking to eat supper, both were hungry. Rachel had long since gone to bed mad, making up her mind to ignore any ruckus associated with homecoming.

"Rach! Come on out here and get us something to eat! You wouldn't let a man starve to death, would you?"

"Go to hell! I don't care if you never eat again. Get your own damn supper!"

(It occurred to me to wonder how Dad could quote verbatim a conversation for which he hadn't been present. In later years I learned from personal experience that these exchanges are pretty much cut and dried.)

"Well, hell, Perry, I guess we're on our own." Pans began to rattle, and the stove lid banged. George must not have been too far gone to put his wits to the problem though. The men began a discussion, just loud enough to be heard by the not sleeping spouse.

166

"Wasn't that the damnedest thing you ever saw?" George asked his companion, who had no doubt been prompted by gestures to play along.

"Yep, sure enough a sight never to be forgotten. It'll make a good story to tell the neighbors."

"Yeah, that plane was so low I was sure it'd crash, but it managed to stay in the air. When it went over that truck, why the ol' boy drivin', he must have thought his time was up, but he never ran off the road."

"What's that? What did you say? Who?"

By now Rachel had tied her robe and approached the stove. *"Go on out of there George, before you burn the eggs."*

"Why, say there Rach. Sorry if we woke you. Go on back to bed."

"Never mind, I'm up now. Sit down and tell me what happened. Start at the beginning."

The tale that unfolded was indeed strange. A small plane, losing altitude, had skimmed the top of a pickup with a stock rack. There was a horse in the back of the truck, and a wing of the plane cut its head right off. The story strung on long enough to get the fellers fed, and Rachel could hardly sleep the rest of the night for needing to get on the party line and spread the news.

Actually, the story was an embellishment of a plane crash that had happened north of Seneca earlier that day. George and his companion had been hauling a horse in the back of a pickup after having oiled themselves pretty nicely. They decided to return to town to replenish the supply, where they heard of the crash.

167

I don't know how long before she found out that the late version was a tall tale that George invented to get himself and his compadre fed, but in Rachel's defense, she told the story on herself many times over. Probably figured the menfolk would keep it going for years anyhow. She'd be right about that, and they didn't even need a phone line to do it. Some of the most interesting conversations happen in the saloon.

Take it on Faith

The snow began as we ate our dinner, but dinner was late that Sunday because the feeding took longer when old drifts had crusted over during brief thaws, and the horse's feet had to be doctored after they were put up. The wind rose too, making the day seem even more unfriendly, and the temperature had hovered around zero all day.

Dad decreed the dishes would wait; that Mom should prepare to leave for Thedford so I wouldn't miss any school. Mom almost never left the dishes, and knowing that a pile of them would be waiting for her when we returned to the ranch on Friday she was reluctant to begin contributing to the mess now. Dad was a good cook, but his kitchen skills ended there.

Nevertheless, we hurried. Dad filled the gas tank while we gathered our things. He brought the car around as Mom hurriedly stacked dishes in the sink but, when we started out the door, Dad announced he'd drive us as far as the Box T, two miles to the east. It made sense. Mom was an uncertain driver at best, and the hill over east would be drifted in, as well as the sharp corner at the bottom before the meadow began. No doubt we'd have been stuck before reaching our nearest neighbor for help.

I loaded extra coats and blankets in the trunk, and made sure the scoop shovel was there. Suddenly, the little blue Chevy looked untrustworthy to me, and I wished we owned a pickup, maybe a Jeep, like the one Merzes had. Something with 4 wheel drive. But the Chevy was it. Since Dad still fed, and put up hay, with horses, there wasn't even a tractor on the place.

We eased out onto the trail road. Gusts of wind decreased visibility as the ground blizzard got going. Drifts grew quickly, outstripping even our anxiety. Dad opened gates and broke trail on the meadows, avoiding the hill, and cuts already closing in, pulling back onto the main road at the shed pasture, where the Box T buildings could be seen through occasional lulls in the storm.

"You should be ok to the highway now. Give 'er hell along the trees there south of Brownlee. It'll be a long drift, but likely not very deep."

That was all. Not "goodbye, good luck," or, "I hope you make it." He shut the car door firmly, with help from the wind, as Mom slid under the wheel, then turned his back and began walking for home. I watched him trudge away, his fur lined cap pulled low, ear flaps tied under the chin, and a scarf on the lower part of his face. Bib overalls over his wool pants and long johns, two coats, chopper mittens on his hands, all of it already coated with snow. Insulated coveralls wouldn't come on the scene for a decade or more.

Mom gritted her teeth and "gave 'er hell," never looking back.

We made the highway without incident, if you discount Mom's nervous tears and shaking hands, and were in Thedford before dark. The image of my dad disappearing into the storm has remained with me these sixty odd years. He would have gone into the house, lit the kerosene lamps, built up the fire and hung his wet clothing near the stove to dry, but not until he'd gone to the barn, fed the horses and milked the cows.

I assume all this, but there's no way to know. With no phones, he had to take it on faith that we'd reach our destination, just as we did that he'd make it home. Just as all of us did; that the sacrifices made to educate ranch kids in those days would pay off. Today, I realize that for non-church goers, we all had a lot more faith than we gave ourselves credit for.

My Career as Teacher's Pet

I spent the years from age four to six campaigning to convince my parents that formal education was unnecessary. The fact that my mother was a former teacher, and my father nursed an enormous regret for having to leave school in ninth grade, should have given me a clue that the battle was useless, but I remained oblivious. The folks ignored my relentless whining and let it be known that four years of college were in my future, as well. College was a dim concept to my little brain but, feeling an obligation to head that off at the pass, I redoubled my efforts, albeit to no avail. We had the same discussion during my senior year in high school, with similar results.

Since our country district had no school, September of 1946 found me firmly ensconced at Grandma Spencer's home in Seneca, and in Mrs. Walsh's first grade class. I hadn't even learned the names of the other kids in my room when, due to a year of home instruction at Mom's behest, I was promoted to second grade. It may have been at the very next recess that I first heard the words, "Teacher's Pet," and deduced the term wasn't meant in a complimentary manner.

From that day on, I withdrew from any voluntary participation in class, but the jig was up because, after incorrect responses from two or three other students, the teacher always called on me and, nine times out of ten, I knew the answer. The exceptions generally occurred in arithmetic. One might assume that my miserable showing in regard to things mathematical would have tempered my peers' opinions about any favored status with faculty, but small minds, once made up, are not easily changed. I, of all people, should have realized this.

Elizabeth made second grade bearable. Actually, she kept me together for the rest of our school years. Aveys lived at the base of the Seneca hill, far enough on the fringes of town to be almost country. Elizabeth was the oldest of five, tall for her age, pretty, in a quiet sort of way, and as much a loner as me. Although two years older, and a better than average student, she was in my class. It never occurred to me to ask why she was behind, I was just grateful to have her. Always last to be chosen for games at recess, we hung out in shared misery. After school she generally had to hurry home, but in summer we spent days at a time in one another's homes. We both loved horses, books, and any activity that required being outdoors. Her mom treated me like one of the brood and, for a lonely only, that was priceless.

For a long time, it was the two of us against the world, but then the country school that our neighbors attended closed, and their clans migrated to town during the week. Wendell and Marjorie Merz, and Percy and Vivian Miller bought homes in Mullen, Lou and Dorothy Merz in Seneca. Now, Dottie hung out with us too, but Shirley had her own group of companions. We picked up a few stray girls who came to town; however, many of those connections were brief, as the families moved on.

Boys were incidental to us. Most were too ornery, too young, or too bratty to be considered, and they never seemed to need one another the way we did. There was an occasional odd man out, like Charles Robinson, who might come to school, when he bothered at all, smelling of the skunk he had trapped on the way there, or Larry Merz, whose learning disabilities afforded him no playmates beyond those of us who associated with his sisters. Most boys simply ran with whoever happened along on any given day and dreamed up whatever scheme seemed least likely to precipitate dire consequences. Along about sixth grade, the genders began to interact and, at least, tolerate one another.

This sort of camaraderie was all that kept me from running away to join the gypsies or some other hair brained scheme that might allow me to forego the need of formal education. Every moment in the classroom was spent resentfully, although I liked my teachers, enjoyed learning and, in spite of efforts to the contrary, got good grades. But none of what I was learning seemed connected to real life, which to me concerned land, livestock, and physical labor. To this day I can't explain my faulty reasoning, other than a natural dislike of being told I had to do something.

I knew better than to voice any of this but it simmered under the surface until the end of my sophomore year when Dad decreed I would now be attending Thedford High since there were more opportunities in a larger school. I fought bitterly, and lost, as I always would where education was concerned, but the dilemma was solved for me when Seneca High School closed at the end of the year. My association with Elizabeth changed then, because she rode the bus to Thedford for our last two years, while Mom got an apartment in Thedford, just a couple of blocks from my new school.

Dottie Merz' class was the last to graduate from Seneca. She had gone on to business school in Lincoln. Elizabeth and I made friends among our new classmates, all of them from the country, all outcasts; nothing new there. Another thing that didn't change was my effort to not graduate at the head of my class. The valedictorian had to make a speech, something to be avoided at all costs. Late in my senior year, after being informed the salutatorian also had to speak, I ended up begging for advice from Shirley Devine, the girl I had most disliked during my Seneca school years.

Someone put out the word that we should stay out all night on graduation. I haven't a notion who, or why; none of us would have done it, even if allowed. After all, what was there to do in Thedford, Nebraska after midnight?

Mom got wind of the rumor and came down on me in no uncertain terms. We were already at odds; me resentful of having to make that speech, wishing I could skip graduation altogether, and fighting over what I would wear under my graduation gown. She decreed I should have a new dress. I wanted nothing in my closet to remind me of school, the distasteful event, or any of the last dozen years. Eventually, she let me wear a dress of hers that I admired.

I got through the ceremonies in a blur, escaped the receiving line earlier than proper, and refused a ride to the apartment. My classmates were engaged in tearful farewells, and lingering promises, of which I wanted no part. In lieu of an all-nighter, the class had agreed to meet at the city park for a bonfire, just hang out for a while, and roast some hot dogs. My parents agreed to this as long as I was home by ten.

I changed into jeans and walked slowly to the park, where some of the kids were tending a fire and setting out food. I suppose our class sponsors were there, we wouldn't have been allowed to organize an official event without adults. I can't even say if all of our class had put in an appearance, but it seems unlikely because, what would the parents of Seneca or country students have done meanwhile? No family had more than one automobile, and none of my class owned any wheels. I do remember that my steady boyfriend, who had just graduated from Mullen High, came to the ceremony, along with his family, but they would have left for home right afterward.

My classmates, or at least those present, stood around awkwardly with not much to say. I ate a hotdog and looked at faces that had been part of my everyday world. Suddenly they all seemed like strangers, or perhaps I had become someone I barely knew. I slipped into the dark and walked to the apartment. The clock struck nine as I opened the door.

"Let's go to the ranch, I said. "I don't want to spend another night in town."

174

May Basket

Shirley Devine was the last person I would have chosen to present with a May Basket. In the first place, she was stuck up. She and her best friend Charlene didn't have the time of day for me and my pals. It's ever thus, concerning the vast separation between third and fourth grade girls, but none of us knew that at the time.

In the second place, Shirley was a blue-eyed blonde, with naturally curly hair. What's not to hate about that, if you're all arms and legs, and skinny, with mouse brown braids?

In the other place, she was smart, probably the only kid in the classroom consisting of third, fourth, and fifth grades, who got better marks than me.

My friends and I spent the last week of April concocting colorful baskets out of cut down cereal boxes, crepe paper, and glitter, and attaching pipe cleaner handles. That part was fun. It must have been a parent who supplied the sweet treats that went into the baskets, since none of us had any visible means of acquiring financial independence.

We made baskets for all the girls in our room. My mom was rigid when it came to not leaving anyone out. However the assignment of who would deliver a basket to which house was accomplished, several small ambassadors of good will were set loose on the village early on that May Day morning.

The May Basket tradition went like this. You went to the door of a house, knocked, quickly put your basket on the porch, and ran away as fast as possible. The intended recipient, who was likely watching from a window, would tear out after the delivery person in an effort to deliver a thank you kiss. We suspected that it would be a lot more exciting if the person trying to catch us was a boy, but were realistic enough to know that no self-respecting male of our own age would be caught dead kissing a girl, even if we'd been allowed to invite such behavior.

It was all fine until we arrived at Shirley's house. Somehow I was designated to knock while my companions stood across the street to make sure this was done correctly. Suddenly, I was breathing hard, even before I'd started to run. Maybe that's why Shirley caught me so quickly, despite the fact that her legs were shorter and she was pleasingly plump. I don't think I wiped her kiss off my cheek. Hopefully I wasn't *that* mean spirited. I do think Shirley was pleased, as she turned back to the little sod house where she lived with her mother and three siblings. Whether or not she received more than one basket I don't know, but three or four awaited me on the porch of Grandma's home. It took years for me to realize some things about the discrepancies in Shirley's and my circumstances, and to be ashamed of my attitude.

May Day customs have disappeared into the mists of time, but this tradition still works. Do something nice for someone and try not to get caught.

Henry

Henry gave me cowboy boot earrings for my high school graduation. They were carved from wood, with sparkly blue stones in the center of a star on the boot tops, and reminded me of fancy styles I used to beg Dad to order in the Blucher catalog.

Whatever became of those earrings? I would never have given or thrown them away, but I don't even know when they disappeared. Sort of like Henry, when he drifted out of my life.

Henry was a strange bird. His eyes had a wild look; the gray gaze shifted on you, then away, as if looking for an escape route, a look I grew to recognize years later as a mental health worker. He reminded me of a bronc, undecided whether to buck or bolt, rear, or roll, always unpredictable. The man likely needed to be on medication, although in those days mental illness went untreated, outside of institutions.

But it wasn't a big deal; everyone just knew Henry was "a little crazy." He floated around the country working here and there, and probably stayed longer at our place than most. My dad felt sorry for Henry, but he wouldn't have lasted long with us if he hadn't been a good worker.

The only thing that riled Dad about the situation was writing Henry's check to his sister. Clara and her husband were salt of the earth folks who no doubt had Henry's best interests at heart, but Dad hated the way Henry never had money of his own; only what was doled out to him for cigarettes, a paperback western, or new jeans, and gas for the rattletrap car he drove to his sister's house on Saturday nights so she could do his laundry. When he left our yard, check in hand, Dad shook his head and growled that a man in mid-life deserved more respect.

Henry was clean, polite, and quieter than most of our hired

hands, except when telling about the adventures of the Daltons, Younger Brothers, James gang, or Doc Middleton. He read a lot and was fascinated with outlaw tales; understandable, for someone who hasn't much personal freedom.

There was this other thing about Henry. He loved to dance, and was good at it. I was a wallflower until the last couple of years of school, when I acquired a steady boyfriend, but I could depend on a dance with Dad, and the dads of friends, as well as a hired man or two, if he was appropriately sober. Those men, including my boyfriend, were all good dancers, but none was as smooth as Henry. He'd show up, hand outstretched to me, every time the band struck up *Rock Around the Clock*, and I didn't care a whit what my friends thought of me out there, cutting a rug with a wild eyed, gray haired old guy.

"Who was that?" a classmate asked, after one of our capers.

"Oh, that's just Henry," I said. "He works for my dad."

I didn't know what became of Henry until recently, when I encountered two of his nieces and inquired. They told me that some years after leaving our community he took his own life.

I think of those pretty earrings often. Maybe I give Henry too much credit for finding something that would please a skinny tomboy who was part outlaw, like the heroes in his dime novels. Possibly his sister picked them out. But no, the look of satisfaction when I opened the box and put them on; I get it now. For once, he had done something on his own.

It's a bittersweet memory, Henry swinging me out on the dance floor, both of us conscious of nothing but the rhythm. So long ago, when I believed that easy kind of joy would last forever, and he took happiness by the hand when the music began, knowing it never does.

All the Way Home

The summer after high school graduation was mostly about denial. I fell into the routine of ranch life as if I'd never have to leave, despite having won a scholarship to Chadron State College and my parents seeing to it that all the necessary paperwork was sent to assure my enrollment in September. Dad had paid me hired man's wages for the summers of my high school years, with the understanding that the money was to be saved for college. But all those preparations seemed like a dream that happened to someone else.

Reality began to sink in late in the summer when I began using the sewing machine my folks had given me for graduation to fashion a wardrobe for college. I could have gone to any of the state colleges, and my mother favored Peru, because that was her alma mater. But it was east, as were Kearney and Wayne. If I had to go to college, and it was evident by now that this was another educational battle I would not win, then I would exercise what little choice I had to strike a westward course.

I never saw the college campus, had never, in fact, been to Chadron, until the day my parents drove me there to begin classes. It seemed impossibly large and I felt even more lost than the day I stepped into Mrs. Walsh's primary room in Seneca. I was furious and frightened all the time I stumbled through registration and class selection. The enrollment that year reached a record high of six hundred students, and everyone but me seemed to know what they were doing and where to go.

With no desire to do anything unrelated to livestock, I was at a loss to choose a course of study. Agriculture wasn't a career option for women in the nineteen fifties. Most of my girl classmates had taken a position teaching country schools. You could do that for one year, right out of high school, provided you had taken normal training classes, and I had. That was enough to tell me I didn't want to teach. At a loss, I settled on a major in home economics. After all, I'd likely marry someday, probably after my current boyfriend finished his military stint. Meanwhile, I'd just mark time.

Before long, a group of country girls formed a pack, much as we had done all through school. We had good times, though none of us dated or joined any clubs. Some had jobs but, due to my scholarship and savings I didn't need to, so there was more time to socialize. By mid-winter I had met a man from Valentine who was back in school after having served in the Navy. Bob DeNaeyer had been briefly married, divorced, and was eager to settle down and raise a family, and he wanted to get back to ranching. The call of home and the hills was too strong to resist, so a Dear John letter went to my soldier boyfriend, and a diamond ring appeared on my hand. We married the next summer, and a few months later he was working for my dad on the home place. I'm sure that my parents were heartbroken that I didn't finish college, but they accepted they had finally lost the educational battle.

No doubt they told each other that I'd be sorry someday, for not getting a degree, and as usual, they were right. But love is blind and deaf, and so is youth.

Will Dad's Boots Fit?

The river flowed faster then. A growing family, ranch responsibilities, and community involvement made the years blur. At times the current shifted, much like the bottom of the Middle Loup, and there were quicksand bogs that made me wonder if the obstacles were unsurmountable. Following a path set forth by my mom and the other women I'd known growing up was comfortable, for the most part, and certainly familiar. This was about as close as I was going to come to my life goals.

As our kids grew older, we all began working together, and although there was hardly a moment to breathe between long hayfield or horseback days and getting meals and garden chores done, it felt like I finally fit somewhere.

On a long ago day when I was about five years old, someone had asked what I wanted to be when I grew up. I recall thinking it was a dumb question, but responded, "A cowboy."

Everyone laughed. Even a five year old knows when they have put their foot in it, and I never again voiced that dream, even to myself. Obviously, it was impossible. But now I was almost there. Good enough.

Dad died suddenly at the age of eighty. Bob was already terminally ill, and I began to realize whose shoulders this cowboy life was about to fall upon. I began keeping notes of everything ranch related: when we weaned, changed pastures, haying rotations, feed rations, even the dates of branding and turnout. Be careful what you wish for; sometimes you get it.

I remembered, as a kid, clomping around the kitchen of our tiny house in Dad's boots. They were too big, but I didn't care. Now they were still too big, and I had better care because a lot of lives depended on how I wore them.

We made it, with a lot of prayer and good help, until the next generation took up the mantle. After being widowed, I was faced with a choice. Stay home, while moving aside to let the younger generation manage ranch decisions, driving my mom to church and gradually becoming one of those rocking chair grannies, or finish my obligation to the parents who dreamed of a college degree for their only child.

Strange that I finally became willing to fit the mold my parents sought for me; the one I fought so valiantly. It has been an adventure, to say the least. The river doesn't always go where you think it will and the scenery changes quickly. Sometimes you fall in a hole over your head, but I've learned to float, if not to swim very well.

Tender Mercies

We don't always get what we deserve, and that is where mercy enters the picture. My insistence on clinging to the familiar, and avoiding risk whenever possible, might well have set me up for failure in a mid-life decision to begin a second career. Instead, stepping over the edge of resistance and fear brought rewards I should have enjoyed much earlier in life. But I have come to believe that nothing happens by mistake. Learning to read body language of animals and the predictions of sky and wind served me well when working with the mentally ill. Learning to accept Larry Merz as a person, rather than an oddity, made it easy for me to relate with folks who had developmental issues.

I knew from the time I learned to read that there were stories inside me, but when people I trusted laughed at the notion I'd ever be a cowboy, my inmost thoughts and dreams got sealed away. Writing meant that you'd know who I was and that knowledge would give you the power to hurt me. But some of us are born to write, so I became a closet writer. At some point, it became more important to share some thoughts with a friend who was hurting than to protect myself, or perhaps, upon reaching our fifties, some of us become braver. At any rate, coming out of that closet brought me a world of like-minded friends, one of whom invited me to share his life.

The Messersmith name has been legendary in the cattle business, so when I met Bruce Messersmith our similar backgrounds and values, created an easy acquaintance, but poetry and music clinched the deal. As we traveled the West to participate in festivals and gatherings of our fellow artists, he often went up to featured performers after an event and introduced himself, asked about their work, and shared some of his own. I hung back, sure that someone so well-known wouldn't want to meet another face in the crowd, but Bruce drew me forward and introduced me, as well. I learned that those folks put their pants on one leg at a time too, and many of them have become dear friends and mentors.

Many of my friends who have remarried have endured family opposition, but my extended family, including former in-laws, have embraced Bruce and our new life together.

It began at that moment when we were getting the marriage license in Elko, Nevada. The man ahead of us was being issued his dog license. Bruce turned to me and said, "Gee, I never realized you go to the same place to get a marriage license and a dog license." I married him anyway, and have never looked back.

Funeral Potatoes, Jello, and Other Culinary Delights

I come from meat and potato country. It's customary to work from dawn to dark, or beyond, now that we have lights in the barn. Before electricity came down the valley, people labored until starlight or whenever the lamp oil ran low. That lifestyle burns a lot of calories, so no one worried about overdosing on mashed potatoes made with real butter or cream puffs the size of saucers. When I was growing up, red meat was on the table three times a day but, except for sowbelly, most of it was plenty lean. Every cook had a meat hammer in the kitchen drawer for pounding steaks, and getting roast cooked tender was a half day project.

We ate a balanced diet, what with vegetables from the garden in summer and the rows of quart jars that testified to hours over a pressure canner. Mom put up corn, beans, peas, and all manner of fruit, as well as our own beef, but there weren't a lot of salads on the table.

I was introduced to salad when we visited my Omaha grandparents. Grandma James' dishes all matched, which in itself, was foreign to me. Her small side plates held a lettuce leaf topped with half a pear, a spoonful of cottage cheese, and for special occasions, a maraschino cherry. There were variations on the theme, but the basic lettuce leaf was a given. Topping might be a tomato slice, pineapple rings, or daintily arranged apricots, but cottage cheese or mayonnaise was ever present. I believed, and do to this day, that cottage cheese resembled something left too long in the sun, and it needed to go into the bucket reserved for chicken scraps. I ate salad rarely, and only under duress.

At the ranch we favored dishes never encountered at my urban relative's tables. Pickled pigs feet were prepared just as ancestors from the old country had done, placed in heavy crocks, covered over with gobs of gelatinous goo, and kept in a cool corner of the cellar. Close behind butchering time, pickled heart and tongue were put down in a separate crock. Cracklings, left over from rendering lard, were popular with many, and the Merz clan favored tripe. You couldn't fault them for that, given their strong German heritage, but I never had the guts to try it.

Dad had enough German in him to enjoy sauerkraut, so in the fall there was usually a crock of that in our pantry. Horseradish was a favorite, too; after all, the meat needed all the help we could give it. Mom hated preparing horseradish even worse than making sauerkraut, so that was generally Dad's deal.

We kids ate our watermelon in thick slices, dripping juice down our chins, off elbows, and onto the grass, if we had been encouraged to take it outdoors. But that was rare, because of our propensity to engage in seed fights, which degenerated into throwing the rinds at one another instead of bringing them in to be cut up and pickled.

Our mothers pickled pretty much anything they had extra; beets, cucumbers, green beans, crabapples, and peaches. By contrast, the store-bought gherkins on Grandma James' formal table seemed a poor substitute. I never heard tell of cantaloupe until encountering it in Omaha, but it looked no different to me than the muskmelon from our ranch garden, which we always raced to harvest before the coyotes did.

Jello was a dish common in both country and city homes. It was likely born in the city, but became popular in our area as a status symbol. Bringing Jello dessert or salad to the pot luck or church supper meant you could afford a refrigerator. Mom was among the last to own such a convenience, which may have been the reason she developed a slobbering love affair with Jello. She wouldn't have used that term; unladylike, not to mention unappetizing. All the same, she would have served Jello for breakfast if she'd thought Dad would put up with it. She made Jello long before we had a refrigerator, putting it in jars to set in the cold water of our milk house tank, or in winter, in the pantry, where anything that could freeze often did.

Rocky Mountain Oysters are listed on upscale city menus these days, but we just called them calf fries and ate them roasted over the branding fire, breaded, or with scrambled eggs. Dad liked calf brains with his eggs too. The DeNaeyers had a taste for head cheese, and my mother-in-law had a standing order at the Valentine locker to save hog heads for her on butcher days. Bob like his mother's beef kidneys, and when I asked her how to prepare them she told me to just boil the pee out of them.

Despite years of ranch wife life, odds were about even, on any given day, whether my mom would burn the biscuits. It wasn't necessarily her fault. The coal range that served as both a heating and cooking source had a temperament all its own. Mom hadn't much cooking practice when she married. Nothing in her upbringing would have prepared her for the everyday chore of feeding half a dozen hungry hands and a husband who had honed his culinary skills by batching from the age of fourteen.

To his credit, after teaching his bride the basics, like boiling water and how to separate an egg, Dad never complained when a meal came out crispy. His deal was frugality, so it seemed preferable to eat what was set before him rather than wasting ingredients on do-overs.

Dad came by his tolerance honestly, I suppose. His own mother's mantra in regard to breakfast toast was, "Burn some bread and scrape it off." I've tinkered with that method myself, and find it acceptable, as long as the scraping process isn't observed by those to whom the toast is served.

Burning biscuits is a trick all rural women know, and I have served my share of them. It's connected with the husbandly request to, "Come here and help me, will you honey? This will only take a minute." Mothers often over-brown biscuits while refereeing a bout of sibling rivalry and that has happened to me, but more often when I try to cook while reading. True to Granny's training, my biscuits sometimes arrive at the table missing the bottom half.

Country cooks of my acquaintance took pride in their culinary specialties, but were always up for variety. When someone brought a new dish to a branding, the recipe went home with every housewife present, and the current favorite was served up until every husband and hired hand up and down the valley began turning it down. Since all were on the edge of poverty, wasted ingredients were unacceptable, and that entrée would be abandoned in favor of something new that someone brought to the funeral dinner last week.

I was recently made aware that rural traditions have traveled uptown as I stood in line at the supermarket behind a woman who was unloading cartons of sour cream, frozen hash browns, and grated cheese from her cart. "Oh," said the checkout clerk, "I see you're making funeral potatoes."

We Are the Sum of Our Ancestors

"Lay your hands on the table," Lee said.

My cousin placed his hands alongside mine and, after a moment of silence said, *"They're Spencer hands, aren't they? Look how square they are, fingernails short, and knuckles gnarled from all the years of hard labor."*

"Don't forget the age spots," I added.

Lee Spencer is the grandson of my dad's brother, Claude, who lived most of his adult life in the Big Horn country of Wyoming. Although Lee and I are the same age we didn't meet until I was ten, when Dad took us on our one and only family vacation to Shell and Greybull, to visit his brothers. Lee and I corresponded for the next decade or so but lost touch during the years of marriage, parenting, and making our way in the world. Recently, I had ferreted out his location and called to see about stopping by while we were in Casper.

Now, this evening of catching up on the mistakes and magic which have woven our journeys. We covered the milestones of life: careers, families, and places we'd lived. Told stories of the ancestors who connect us, looked at the pictures, and did all the other stuff you do at times like that. But now the strongest evidence of our connection lay on the table before us.

The last time I had seen my cousin he and his father looked enough like my dad to have been the sons Dad never had. Today, he resembles his grandfather, but the four hands spread on the table are those of my grandmother, as I remember her in her eighties.

It was surely a hardscrabble life there on the prairie, with a houseful of children, and more mouths to feed arriving as the years rolled on. Grandmother's hands would have tended the garden in summer and lined shelves with jars of produce to feed them all winter, washed clothes on a board, and tied quilts on a frame in the drafty rooms of that dreary dwelling at the edge of a meadow.

Grandfather's hands I never knew, but I imagine they would have been calloused, chapped, and cracked from the work, with strong fingers that stripped the last milk from warm teats, or clasped the legs of a calf to coax it from the womb. Hands that delivered punishment to errant offspring, signed another promissory note, or stretched wire around property which he claimed as legacy for his heirs.

Their descendants are like them in so many ways: a mannerism, a crooked smile, space between front teeth, artistic talent, or mechanical ability, and a certain stubbornness that won't let us give up on a project or an argument. All these years later, their stories remain in the shape of four hands on a table this night, in a trailer house on the Wyoming plains.

There's a lot that Lee and I didn't share and perhaps have hidden, even from ourselves, but clasping it all, holding us back from the brink of desperation and despair, lifting us to a level we didn't dream of attaining, steadying us, leading us into the jaws of each storm, and soothing us, are generations of these Spencer hands.

My cousin and I adopted the high lonesome as the arena for our competitions. We are a compilation of the selves we chose to see, or not, and the ancestors who set us down in godforsaken country and gave us a star to steer by. Our own sunsets approach now, as we decide what to hold and keep and what to bury in the little country graveyard overlooking a river. None of us ponder these things until there's more daylight behind us than ahead, or when someone asks us to lay our hands on a table.

Family Reunion

My grandson has been to the junk pile. He comes by it honestly. As I child, I spent hours exhuming interesting artifacts from that same dump, as did my own children, one of whom has rescued and restored several pieces of furniture from our past lives. So I wasn't surprised, when I went about the yard work, to find pieces of our family puzzle scattered here and there. My grandson had no idea he was bringing back bits of ancestors he has never met, or wouldn't recognize without the wrinkles.

Two brothers, whose names he carries, are here. The Prince Albert can was my dad's, and my uncle is represented by a whisky flask: symbol of his life and his death.

The dried up nail polish would be Mom's. She fussed over her nails for years, but finally gave up and let the washboard, garden, and heavy work have their say.

Here are Coca Cola bottles—the little ones that we used to return for a refund. Mine, no doubt, although I can't believe they were discarded, because that two cent return was a big deal to me. Soda was a major treat, not an everyday matter.

The vinegar jug must have been Grandma's, left from days of pickling and preserving over a hot coal range. Strange that it never found a second life as water carrier for the hayfield. This bit of colored glass is from a vase of hers. No one else would remember, but I'm the one who broke it, and I cried all afternoon, knowing how she had treasured it.

Pieces of a plate are part of my parents' wedding china. Here is a kind of barbed wire that isn't made anymore, and these wheels are from Tonka trucks my grandson's dad used to play with. Those were some tough toys, but the modern versions are made of plastic, and don't need to last as long because kids

191

today soon gain other interests.

A lard pail is evidence of hundreds of pies baked by Mom. Grandma would have rendered her own lard. Here's a tin cup, the kind with blue speckled enamel, and a pie plate of the same material, with a hole in the bottom. Over there, a broken crock, and a chunk of cast iron from the stove that baked those pies.

Separator discs and a cream can remind me of the cream check that was my allowance in high school years. On a good week, it might amount to three or four dollars—a small fortune, which I made last as long as possible. Even then, there was a lot of my dad in me.

My grandson wouldn't know about any of that. To him it's just fascinating junk. I planned to haul everything back over the hill but, on second thought, used some of it to enhance a flower bed by the steps. Family reunions aren't necessarily attended only by the living.

Channeling Christine

Grandma Spencer used to say I looked like her younger daughter, Christine, who died in the influenza epidemic of 1918. There must be a resemblance because she sometimes called me Christine, in an absent minded moment.

I've always been curious about Christine. Was she pretty? Did she like to dance, tell stories, or love animals? What was it about me that reminded Grandma of her, and why didn't I ask? The single picture I have of Christine is faded and blurred, so her features are undecipherable. The slim figure with upswept hair and floor length skirts, in the fashion of the day, is merely a shadow inviting speculation.

If I had it to do over, I would ask. But for that to happen I'd had to have developed a personality that allowed me to speak out, rather than retreating into confused silences for fear of opening a can of worms that would spread bitterness or sadness. Since that wasn't the case, Christine has remained just another ghost that wanders restlessly through the hills of home.

I know where her homestead was, the place where she lived with her husband, Wilber Nolan, but not how long they lived there or why, after her death, he sold it back to the family and moved on. Did she die alone there, or was her husband at her side? Perhaps her mother came to nurse her? Was my grandmother prostrate with grief, or did she carry on stoically as so many women of her day had done? Perhaps she herself was abed—I never asked how many family members were ill in that epidemic.

I know that Wilbur drank too much and died a few years later in a car accident, never having remarried, but I don't know why he was known sometimes as Wilford Nowland, never mind that Wilbur is on his grave marker. Knowing this family, I can deduce that there's much more to tell, but no one was telling then, and now there's no one left who could.

Why is it that the most fascinating mysteries are those involving people close to us? Perhaps knowing more of Christine's story would have helped me avoid some large lessons and heartaches. On the other hand, if I was really like her, it's likely I wouldn't have asked for advice, any more than I questioned Grandma.

My way of learning is mostly made up of watching from the sidelines and searching for lessons in the details of life. With age and experience in the school of hard knocks, I've become an expert watcher and a better learner, but it's high time I begin asking some questions.

Grandma's Geraniums and a Bit of Blue Glass

On a warm September day I cut back and re-potted geraniums that graced the deck all summer. Brought them to the sunny south room and breathed in the spicy scent that always transports me to Grandma Spencer's dining room, where geraniums brightened a bench in her south window.

I cared little for geraniums in childhood, preferring wild flowers or the showy peonies in my Omaha grandmother's yard. Frankly, I cared little for anything about Grandma Spencer's house, because she wasn't exactly the "read a story, rock you to sleep" type. Looking back, I realize she indulged us in plenty of other ways, and exhibited more patience than should be required of a woman in her eighth decade, whose life had been anything but easy. We youngsters were allowed to bang loudly and tunelessly on the piano in her parlor. We raced 'round her dining table until the pattern in her rug grew dim, pulled linens from the hall closet to make a playhouse, played hide and seek in the dirt floored basement, and ate all the crabapples off her tree.

A few years ago, Fran Pearman Dwyer, an artist, whose people were neighbors of my grandparents, gave me one of her lovely paintings of a pot of red geraniums, so lifelike I can almost smell them. I hung it in the ranch kitchen and become a child again whenever I look at it.

It's November now, and my potted geraniums are in bloom again, a link to times that seemed unremarkable then, but shaped the woman I became. On the window sill above the plants, a bit of blue glass reflects the light. The jagged fragment from some ancient perfume bottle or salt shaker caught my eye as I mowed the yard last summer, and took me back to our chilly bedroom where I used to remove the cap from Mom's small bottle of *Evening in Paris* cologne and take in a deep breath that conjured up exotic evenings, not in Paris, but the Seneca dance hall.

My friends and I had the good fortune not to realize our limited circumstances. Our toys were simple ones, but we liked them. What we liked more was digging in a sandy corner in what passed for yards in that time and place. We carved out roads and forts, shaped wet sand into houses and barns, and populated our villages with families of marbles, pretty stones, or bits of colored glass. Colored glass has always drawn my attention, and I kept one of Mom's cast-off cologne bottles among my treasures. None of our cleverly crafted educational toys can deliver the hours of enjoyment that was provided by our imaginations and remnants from the junk pile.

So I stopped the mower and pocketed the bit of blue glass. It's my key to a time when we believed we could create for ourselves a world well grounded, safe, and predictable. If we all still believed that, might it truly be possible?

Of this much I am sure. When I smell the geraniums and view the morning through a bit of blue glass, that sense of innocence and hope returns, and I know how wise we used to be.

No Roof But Sky

I come from a long line of sky watchers. My maternal grandparents were city dwellers all their lives, yet some of my earliest memories are of Grandpa taking me out in the backyard of their Omaha home to see the moon or wish on a star. He watched the calendar like a kid counting off days until Christmas and celebrated each full moon as eagerly as a lovesick youth, and the tendency lives on in me.

As livestock producers, Dad's people naturally read sky as faithfully as the evening paper, so it's no wonder that I can barely be in a room with curtains drawn. The first thing I do every morning is look out the window at the sky, and upon waking in the night, my eyes search out a star.

All of us need some sort of reminder that many aspects of our universe are larger, more mysterious and miraculous than the everyday events. Sky watching forces us to consider that our concerns are only a small part of a plan that's been in place before we were even a thought.

My mother knew this. She never was an outdoorsy person, didn't garden or tend the yard and certainly didn't care to haul food out to share with the ants at a picnic, but she liked sitting on the porch at sundown or scanning the Milky Way. When her vision deteriorated to the point where driving herself to social occasions was impractical, it made sense for her to retire in town. She enjoyed being able to socialize more, but complained that streetlights made it impossible to see the stars. Every time she was able to spend a night in the country, she looked upward to see if they were all still in place.

Not long before her death, she mentioned being up at three in the morning. I inquired whether she had been ill, or simply couldn't sleep.

"Neither," she replied. "I heard on the radio that there would be a power outage from two to five, so I set my alarm and went outside to see if I could still see the stars."

Secrets

We stopped pretending my mother wasn't dying on the third day that she lay propped in the hospital bed, her tiny frame slowly melting away under the sheet. That day, the director of her assisted living facility had been to visit, leaving in tears after tenderly telling Mom that her apartment would be waiting if she needed to enter the nursing home for a while.

Mom would have done anything to stay out of a nursing home, up to and including dying. Until that moment, she was probably the only one of us who believed there was a possibility she would leave the hospital alive, but with the nursing home option on the table she prepared to avoid that scenario in the only way she could.

Not that she said as much. We knew by the way she stopped caring whether any of us sat with her around the clock, and in fact, began urging us, in a voice that barely qualified as a whisper, to go home and rest. We took the advice, one by one, and those whose turn it was to watch spent more time roaming the halls, so as not to worry her.

Gradually, we began asking her things that had seemed inconsequential before. Where she and Dad went on their first date, how she learned to drive on our country roads, and the secret to those chocolate chip cookies that we had all tried, unsuccessfully, to duplicate. In answer to the latter she smiled weakly and said, "Lots of cussing." We smiled, in turn, at this from a woman who had barely said 'damn' in all of her ninety five years.

We told her she couldn't leave us without specific instructions, but her smile faded, as we joked about keeping secrets from us and wondered how we'd manage to survive without those cookies, though she hadn't baked in years. In truth, there was no secret recipe, only ineptness on our parts.

It was one of my daughters-in-law who asked about the early years, sometime in those last days. Wasn't it hard, coming out West, dealing with different customs and having to make do with so little? Had she ever considered it a mistake?

"My mother told me I could come home anytime I wanted," Mom replied. "I burned the letter."

And all your bridges, I wanted to say, but didn't. Her secret felt like a physical blow to me, but resentment which began to smolder in my gut must remain my own secret. I had wasted my youth conniving and scheming to keep her from leaving us, only now discovering that she'd made up her mind to lie in the bed of her mistakes years ago.

The least she could have done was tell us.

A Backward Glance

The congregation didn't half fill the little church of my childhood, because most folks who knew the deceased have gone on ahead of him. Still, the pastor had her work cut out in getting us to sit down and shut up so the memorial service could begin. We had grown up knowing the inside of one another's homes, the foibles of various sets of parents and grandparents, the names of a few dozen pets, which family cars were apt not to start on cold mornings, and who wouldn't eat oatmeal but craved green olives.
A bunch of wild haired hoodlums, we played ball by our own rules, climbed every tree that would support our weight, learned to work, dance, and stand up to bullies. So, with all these miles and years between, we had a lot of catching up to do.

Likely none of us imagined that Larry would be the one to unite us in this way, as we reveled in memories, brushed aside an occasional tear, indulged in chuckles and belly laughs, shared stories of what we've survived and how we managed to come through it all in one piece. We've been reunited at other times and places over the years, for our parents' milestone celebrations, and to bury them, but this seemed different. Larry was of our generation, and it's sobering to look around and wonder who won't be back for the next gathering of clans.

If Larry had been in our midst, he'd have been smiling. He'd have sat to one side and observed, wouldn't have said much, entering into the conversation when invited, but mostly content to be with family, friends, and neighbors. Just one of the neighborhood kids, as we were growing up, he was along for the ride, and glad to be. His lifelong challenges are part of our collective stories: they helped to shape our perceptions of the world and the manner in which we've responded to our own limitations, and those of others.

Over time, as we watched his family play the hand they were dealt with grace and good cheer; the siblings, cousins, and playmates caught some of that. Self-pity and mean spiritedness weren't tolerated by the adults who had charge of us. We were expected to do our best, according to our abilities, and to treat everyone the same. As I looked around the church, I realized we've become our parents: the kind of people who sign up for the long haul, look out for one another, and meet life on life's terms. That has played out in many ways, from starting businesses, raising grandchildren, caring for siblings, parents, or spouses as they became more dependent, or simply deciding to take the road less traveled and discover what lies around the bend.

Most of those present were on the shady side of fifty. Our lives haven't turned out as we imagined they would, but when asked how we're holding up against adversity, we'll tell you it's going to be just fine, and we mean it.

With every passing day, I'm more aware of how blessed we were to be born to the parents we had, in the community where we lived, in the era when we grew to maturity. We had everything money can't buy, and just enough of the things it can. We had Larry to teach us that no one is really all that different, and we had one another. In our hearts, we still do.

It Won't Wash Off

There's no horsehair on my Wranglers today. Not a trace of blood or birthing fluids on my sleeve, nor recycled grass and water caked on my boots. The windmill oil and wrenches are back in the shop where they belong. There's no mud on the kitchen floor or greasy handprints on the phone. Although the numbers for the vet and implement dealer are still firmly in my mind, someone else makes the calls now. Day by day there's a little less of me, and a lot more memory.

Most of my life has been spent wallowing around in messy situations that left hands and clothing stained with grease, bodily excretions, or leavings from the land. My houses have borne the tracks of that life: dog hair on the carpet and dust on flat surfaces from leaving windows open to catch a breeze or smells and sounds of meadow and corral. Routines begun by ancestors who homesteaded here are as predictable as the seasons, but seasons run together when most of the markers are gone.

The calendar says spring, but it must be wrong. Spring is supposed to surprise me with the cries of Sandhill cranes sliding down the wind while I dig postholes on a hillside, songs of peepers in the meadow when I come in for supper at dusk, and the moon breaking its heart on the surface of a lake ruffled by God's breath.

It can't be spring. My coveralls hang there on a hook in the hallway, and the spotlight rests undisturbed on a shelf. I haven't spent a single hour trying to bring a tiny foot forward inside a mama moaning slightly with each contraction, thumped slimy sides, or breathed into pink nostrils to share my gift of life; haven't walked fences built by my granddad, with a roll of wire on my shoulder and a pocket full of staples.

There's a light in the cow barn tonight, and a night horse tied to the corral fence. A miracle is unfolding under a dim circle of light, in a chilly stall, but I'm not part of it. Someone else's hands, less arthritic than mine, have plunged into the moist warmth, applied steady pressure until a hoof aligned with the nose, and next year's promise burst from the womb.

This night, I finally understand why my dad built his retirement home on a hill overlooking the barn and meadows. I wonder how often he stood here, outside the circle, looking in like a hungry urchin with nose pressed to the window of a candy store. Did he too take coffee on the porch in summer, breathing in meadow mint and fresh cut hay, recalling the clatter of a mower, the jingle of harness, and seeing in his mind's eye fragrant stems falling behind the sickle? When autumn dusk was thick with haze and the sorrow of calves spending their first night away from their mothers, did his heart reach across the years to the man he used to be?

Watching the evening star ride above intense hues of a winter sunset, would he have felt himself trudging toward the milk house with steam rising from foaming pails in either hand?

I suspect Dad was no happier about transitioning into the winter of life than I, but he was quiet about it. Everything I've ever had to let go of has had bloody claw marks all over it. Still, bit by bit, I'm coming to know, as he must have, that the person I am, or always believed myself to be, is disappearing.

Dad never knew a stranger; he was always full of questions, and eager to learn. I've never been much good at getting acquainted with strangers, and this new person in my skin isn't very much help because she's always looking over her shoulder. She's still got a battered Stetson and her spurs hanging on a hook by the door. Bull sales are marked on the calendar and she turned down an invitation to join the women's club last week. She'll likely be that bent old woman at the sale barn, pushing a walker while looking over the newest genetics.

I've tried all manner of things to keep from unraveling: washed my hands, hair, and clothing, blown the dust from my nose and ironed wrinkles from my soul. I've left my heart out in the rain, buried it in a snowdrift, soaked it in ninety-proof, and baked it under an August sun. I've let the wind tear cobwebs away, made promises to the moon and myself, and here's the essence of all that I've gleaned from those tactics.

With us, ranching isn't so much a birthright as a birthmark. Dad must have known it wouldn't wash off. He kept that to himself. Never mind. Some lessons can only be learned as the river carries us along.

Epilogue

What I want to say about growing up in a community where neighbors were people we counted on, didn't judge, and knew inside out, is that it felt safe. We didn't talk to them daily, or even weekly, but I knew they were there, just down the road, around the hill by the lake, or along the road to Seneca.

Looking back, with eyes no longer veiled by innocence, I can imagine that they did, in some manner, judge us. My dad's insistence on doing without electricity and other conveniences likely seemed silly to them, and the women probably felt sorry for my mother. The men may have been baffled at how tight fisted my dad was; how he clung to the old ways. Still, all of them were survivors of the Depression, so perhaps they simply accepted that people have different ways of dealing with fear.

In any event, I never got a sense of being outside the circle. Things and people just were as they were, and life flowed around the details with few ripples or disturbances to mark the progression of days that slipped into years, leaving us barely marked by outward events.

I suppose that is the reason I easily accept people who are different, and made it easier to adjust and use whatever resources are at hand. But the feeling of security blinded me to other aspects of society and made me too trusting, unwilling to assign ulterior motives, or even recognize my own.

Now that the veil of denial is rent and tattered, I sometimes doubt my ability to assess and respond appropriately to challenges. If my perceptions were skewed for all those years, how would I have developed the skills to function as a responsible adult, or even know if there is any gift in me worth sharing?

What I want to say about the journey is that I dived into it, even the trauma and drama. I haven't always, or even very often, been aware of each nuance, or the consequences of my decisions. I haven't given credit where it was due, and have been too quick to assign blame where there was none.

Much of the time I simply took the path of least resistance, and for that I am sorry. But God is good. Whatever mistakes and failures are contained in these threescore and more years there remains the knowledge that once upon a time, I was offered acceptance, and the gift of shining moments.

Someone famous—I forget who—once said that, in spite of how we perceive events, everything really happens all at once. So maybe it wasn't a long time ago, after all.

Acknowledgments

I am grateful, beyond words, for the support and love of the Eatinger, Merz, Miller, Porath, and Avey families, who helped me make sense of a complex world and become a person who is mostly comfortable in her skin. They, and their descendants, are a continuing thread in the lives of my children and grandchildren; a blessing never to be taken lightly.

My parents and grandparents were constantly in my corner, even when I objected. They were wise enough to let me make my own mistakes and live with the consequences. Many teachers recognized my efforts not to excel and encouraged me to put that mindset behind me. It took longer than they hoped, but I take full responsibility for the time lapse.

The DeNaeyer and Messersmith families have opened their hearts to one another. I am eternally grateful that I never had to choose between them.

So many cowboy poets, musicians, writers, and storytellers across the West have been mentors, and shown me that we who share are blessed many times over in return. They are the reason I have dared to put a toe in yesterday's rivers.

My children often said, "Tell about something that happened when you were little." I could never think of anything worth telling. It has taken too long, but now I know it is all worth telling.

Some of these tales appeared in slightly different form in *The Sheridan County Journal Star, The Valentine Midland News*, and *Cattle Business Weekly*. I appreciate the editors who gave me time and space to discover myself.

My trail partner and heart sister, Deb Nolting, has been a

faithful companion on many journeys. It's not easy to find someone who is willing to offer honest and constructive comments on manuscripts. May her tribe increase.

My husband, Bruce, has stuck up for me, stuck by me during all sorts of crises, and believed in me when I couldn't. He is the wind beneath my wings.